New York City's
25Best

by Kate Sekules

Fodor's Travel Publications
New York • Toronto •
London • Sydney • Auckland
www.fodors.com

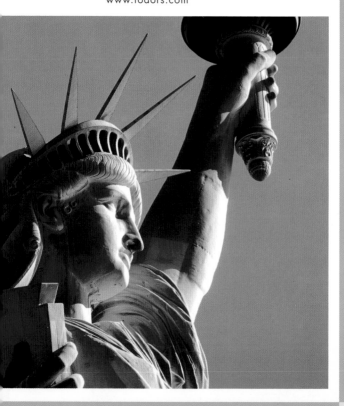

How to Use This Book

KEY TO SYMBOLS

✚ Map reference to the accompanying fold-out map

✉ Address

☎ Telephone number

🕓 Opening/closing times

🍴 Restaurant or café

🚊 Nearest rail station

Ⓜ Nearest subway (Metro) station

🚌 Nearest bus route

⛴ Nearest riverboat or ferry stop

♿ Facilities for visitors with disabilities

❓ Other practical information

▷ Further information

ℹ Tourist information

✋ Admission charges: Expensive (over $10), Moderate ($5–$10), and Inexpensive ($5 or less)

★ Major Sight   ★ Minor Sight

👣 Walks   🚐 Excursions

🏬 Shops

🎵 Entertainment and Nightlife

🍴 Restaurants

This guide is divided into four sections

• Essential New York: An introduction to the city and tips on making the most of your stay.

• New York by Area: We've broken the city into six areas, and recommended the best sights, shops, entertainment venues, nightlife and restaurants in each one. Suggested walks help you to explore on foot.

• Where to Stay: The best hotels, whether you're looking for luxury, budget or something in between.

• Need to Know: The info you need to make your trip run smoothly, including getting about by public transportation, weather tips, emergency phone numbers and useful websites.

Navigation In the New York by Area chapter, we've given each area its own color, which is also used on the locator maps throughout the book and the map on the inside front cover.

Maps The fold-out map accompanying this book is a comprehensive street plan of New York. The grid on this fold-out map is the same as the grid on the locator maps within the book. We've given grid references within the book for each sight and listing.

Contents

Introducing New York

"New York is an island off the coast of Europe." There's a lot of truth in this witticism, and it's no wonder this is the city most overseas visitors choose first. The qualities that weld New Yorkers to the city also mark them out as alien to heartland America.

Residents of Manhattan value directness, diversity and creativity; they live at a ridiculous pace; they work all hours (they have to, to pay the rent); they walk—fast—everywhere; they fail to keep their opinions to themselves; they have street smarts; they are capital L Liberal. Of the so-called Blue States–those dominated by Democrats–New York is the bluest of them all. The city that actually lived through the 9/11 attack that kicked off this era of paranoia and xenophobia, refuses to give into fear; New Yorkers have all the *chutzpah* they ever did.

Here, where some hip neighborhood is forever preparing to eclipse the last hot spot, change is the only constant. The crime-ridden, graffiti-scarred mean streets of the late 20th century are but a distant memory. In fact, terrorist threats notwithstanding, New York remains the safest large city in America, according to the FBI Uniform Crime Report. In stark contrast to the gritty days, you'll see Bugaboo strollers everywhere, because there is a mini baby-boom in progress. Real estate prices are in the realm of fiction, and a whole lot of regular folks have decamped for Brooklyn, while those who can't afford Brooklyn have gone to Queens. Harlem is all glamorous and beautiful; the Bronx is next. Staten Island, the fifth borough that most visitors know only for its fabulous ferry, is the final frontier.

But for many, Manhattan will always be the center of the universe. You can only take in so much of the big picture in one visit. So do as New Yorkers do–find a corner of the city and make it your own.

Facts + Figures

- **Visitors in 2006: 44 million (a record)**
- **Dollars spent by visitors: $24.7 billion**
- **Hotel rooms by end 2007: 72,250**
- **Eating establishments: 18,696**
- **New restaurants in 2006: 222**

REAL ESTATE

The obsession with real estate here easily rivals that of the UK. With prices remaining high and bubble fears–at least at this writing–failing to materialize, the homes of many property-owning New Yorkers are not just their castles, they are their portfolio, retirement plan and chief financial burden.

4

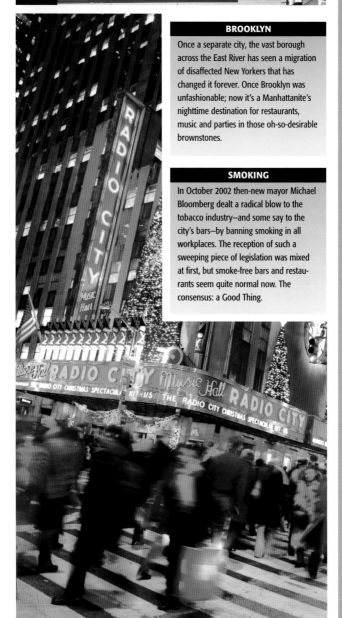

BROOKLYN

Once a separate city, the vast borough across the East River has seen a migration of disaffected New Yorkers that has changed it forever. Once Brooklyn was unfashionable; now it's a Manhattanite's nighttime destination for restaurants, music and parties in those oh-so-desirable brownstones.

SMOKING

In October 2002 then-new mayor Michael Bloomberg dealt a radical blow to the tobacco industry—and some say to the city's bars—by banning smoking in all workplaces. The reception of such a sweeping piece of legislation was mixed at first, but smoke-free bars and restaurants seem quite normal now. The consensus: a Good Thing.

A Short Stay in New York

DAY 1

Morning Begin your day at 8.30 by taking the subway to **Grand Central Terminal** (▷ 58) and having breakfast in the splendid food court. Look at the main hall as you pass slowly through, then exit at 42nd Street and walk east to the **Chrysler Building** (▷ 52). Swing into the lobby, continue east through Tudor City to United Nations Plaza and walk north.

Mid-morning Stroll around the UN gardens by the East River, then take a tour of the **UN General Assembly Hall** (▷ 66). Double back on 42nd Street to Fifth Avenue and look in at the **New York Public Library** (▷ 61).

Lunch If it's summer, get something from the very good kiosks in Bryant Square or sit at one of Bryant Park Café's outdoor tables. In bad weather, eat inside the main restaurant.

Afternoon Walk a block and a half up Avenue of the Americas to the **International Center of Photography** (▷ 65) and after a quick viewing, head another block west to **Times Square** (▷ 63). Explore there, then join a line at the TKTS booth for discounted Broadway tickets.

Mid-afternoon Take Seventh Avenue up to 48th Street and go east, passing through the diamond district, to **Rockefeller Center** (▷ 62). Look around, then continue north up Fifth Avenue, passing St. Patrick's Cathedral to your right. For the rest of the afternoon, either shop **Fifth Avenue** (▷ 56) or head to **MoMA** (▷ 60) half a block west on 53rd Street. Or, if neither appeals, keep going up Fifth to **Central Park** (▷ 74).

Dinner Take up your early reservation at swanky **Lever House** (▷ 70).

Evening Enjoy whichever show you scored discount tickets for.

DAY 2

Morning Have a light breakfast at **Café Sabarsky** (▷ 88) in the Neue Galerie and be at the **Metropolitan Museum of Art** (▷ 80) when it opens at 9.30. Spend a while exploring the galleries.

Mid-morning Go back to the **Neue Galerie** (▷ 84), which opens at 11, and then squeeze in the **Guggenheim** (▷ 78). (Not ideal but at least you'll get a taste.)

Lunch Head over to Madison Avenue to **Jackson Hole** (▷ 88) for a burger, or if it's a beautiful day, leave enough time to enter Central Park at 85th Street and have lunch at the **Boat House** (▷ 88).

Afternoon Take the downtown 6 from 86th Street to Spring Street and do some shopping in SoHo. If shopping's not your thing, stay on the 6 (crossing the platform at Brooklyn Bridge, City Hall to the 4, 5) to Bowling Green, walk through Battery Park and board a ferry to the **Statue of Liberty** (▷ 26) and **Ellis Island** (▷ 25).

Dinner Dine at **Café Gray** (▷ 70) in the Time Warner Center, enjoying the view of the city lights. Or if you thought far enough ahead, take your place at **Per Se** (▷ 70). If you did the latter, that *is* your evening.

Evening Walk up Broadway to **Lincoln Center** (▷ 94). If it's summer, take your dancing shoes to Midsummer Night's Swing on Josie Robertson Plaza; if not watch a performance in one of the many halls. Afterward, take in the late session at **Dizzy's Club Coca Cola** (▷ 99) back at Time Warner.

ESSENTIAL NEW YORK A SHORT STAY IN NEW YORK

These pages are a quick guide to the Top 25, which are described in more detail later. Here they are listed alphabetically and the tinted background shows the area they are in.

UPPER WEST SIDE
89-100

UPPER WEST SIDE

Riverside Park

American Museum of Natural History

Lincoln Center

Hudson

Cooper-Hewitt National Design Museum

Central Park Reservoir

Metropolitan Museum of Art

Central Park

Guggenheim Museum

UPPER EAST SIDE & CENTRAL PARK
71-88

UPPER EAST SIDE

Whitney Museum of American Art

Roosevelt Island

Frick Collection

FIFTH AVENUE

MIDTOWN
49-70

Rockefeller Center

BROADWAY

Times Square

Fifth Avenue

New York Public Library

Museum of Modern Art

MIDTOWN MANHATTAN

Chrysler Building

Grand Central Terminal

Empire State Building

East

DOWNTOWN
35-48

CHELSEA

UNION SQUARE

GRAMERCY PARK HISTORICAL DISTRICT

Union Square

Union Square Park

GREENWICH VILLAGE

Washington Square Park

EAST VILLAGE

NOHO

East River Park

AROUND LOWER MANHATTAN
20-34

SOHO

LOWER MANHATTAN

TRIBECA

Hudson

LITTLE ITALY

CHINATOWN

LOWER EAST SIDE

East

BATTERY PARK CITY

WALL STREET

South Street Seaport

Battery Park

Ellis Island & Statue of Liberty

Brooklyn

ESSENTIAL NEW YORK TOP 25

9

Shopping

Thought there was nothing you couldn't buy over the internet? Think again! New York is a shopping haven, with clothing, furniture, food and souvenirs available no place else. Shopping is still one of the best ways to get an inside look at life in New York—its trends, fads, pace, cultural influences and sense of humor. From massive department stores to small boutiques, the city has something for everyone.

A Piece of New York
You'll find all kinds of NYC paraphernalia—from Statue of Liberty coin banks and taxicab neckties to sweatshirts bearing the New York Police Department initials and Yankee baseball caps. Museum shops offer reproductions, posters, jewelry, stationery and commemorative items.

Fashion
For fashion head for Nolita and SoHo, where small (and often expensive) boutiques line the streets. Major franchises can also be found here, along Broadway, and side streets such as Prince Street, Broome Street and Spring Street. If you're planning a night out on the town, try the stores along 8th Street, starting on Broadway and heading west. These are popular among young clubbers—mannequins in the storefronts flaunt outrageously sexy garb.

ALEXANDER
MCQUEE

Music
Music lovers will find no shortage of places to

Shoes in a SoHo shop; sweet bread in Union Square; designer label in Chelsea; one happy shopper

---

WINDOW SHOPPING

No visit here is complete without window shopping. Start on Lexington between 59th and 60th streets: you'll see the flags outside Bloomingdale's. Walk west to Madison Avenue; between 60th and 61st streets is Barney's, for expensive clothing, jewelry, accessories and beauty products. Walk west along 57th Street, past Chanel and Christian Dior, to the prestigious Henri Bendel and Bergdorf Goodman stores. On Fifth Avenue peer in at Gucci, Tiffany's and Prada.

browse, whether looking for chart-toppers or something from the past. CDs are available at major chain stores such as Virgin. In the Village, smaller music stores carry vintage records, tapes and CDs at prices ranging from a few dollars to several hundred for collectors' editions. Note: DVDs and videos cannot be played on European machines.

Bargains

If you are looking for a bargain, try the popular sample sales, where designer brands are marked down as much as 80 percent. Designer sales are often held at open showrooms over a few days. Arrive early on the first day of the sale for the best selection, though prices do drop as days go by. To learn about sample sales pick up *New York* magazine or *Time Out New York*, or log onto www.dailycandy.com or www.nysale.com. For electronic goods try J & R Music & Computer (✉ 1–34 Park Row ☎ 212/238-9000) or Circuit City (✉ 52 W 14th Street ☎ 212/387-0730), plus other locations.

A Bite to Eat

As for food, in addition to the many upscale restaurants and cafés, simple NYC classics like hot dogs, pizza, bagels and frozen yogurt can be found on nearly every street corner, along with food carts purveying anything from hot soft pretzels or candied almonds to six kinds of curry or falafel sandwiches—great street food.

East Village outlet; Kors on Mercer Street; Dean & Deluca deli; glassware; Macy's at Christmastime

---

FLEA MARKETS

Bric-a-brac is at a premium in New York. You can find everything from silver and beaded jewelry to clothing, artworks and antiques at the Annex Antique Fair & Flea Market (✉ 6th Avenue from 24th to 27th streets), dawn–dusk every weekend, admission $1. Uptown, check out the huge GreenFlea market on Sunday, 10–6 (✉ Columbus Avenue between 76th and 77th streets). There is a Saturday GreenFlea market 11–7 in the Village (✉ Greenwich Avenue and Charles Street).

Shopping by Theme

Whether you're looking for a department store, a quirky boutique, or something in between, you'll find it all in New York. On this page shops are listed by theme. For a more detailed write-up, see the individual listings in New York by Area.

ACCESSORIES

Coach (▷ 68)
Laila Rowe (▷ 97)

BEAUTY

Zitomer (▷ 85)

BOOKS

Applause Theatre and
  Cinema Books (▷ 97)
Barnes and Noble (▷ 97)
Kitchen Arts and Letters
  (▷ 85)
The Mysterious Bookshop
  (▷ 32)

CLOTHES

Abercrombie & Fitch
  (▷ 32)
Barneys (▷ 85)
Bergdorf Goodman
  (▷ 68)
Betsey Johnson (▷ 97)
Brooks Brothers (▷ 32)
Calvin Klein (▷ 85)
Cynthia Rowley (▷ 45)
Donna Karan (▷ 85)
Jeffrey New York (▷ 45)
Malia Mills (▷ 97)

Marc Jacobs (▷ 45)
Paul Smith (▷ 45)
Ralph Lauren (▷ 85)
Resurrection (▷ 32)
Shanghai Tang (▷ 85)
Scoop (▷ 45)
Steven Alan (▷ 97)

DEPARTMENT STORES

Barneys (▷ 85)
Bergdorf Goodman
  (▷ 68)
Bloomingdale's (▷ 85)
Macy's (▷ 68)
Saks Fifth Avenue (▷ 68)
Takashimaya (▷ 68)

DISCOUNT

Century 21 (▷ 32)
DSW and Filene's (▷ 45)
Ina (▷ 32)
Loehmann's (▷ 45)

FOOD AND WINE

Chelsea Market (▷ 45)
Fairway (▷ 97)
Gourmet Garage (▷ 32)
Greenmarket (▷ 45)
Kam Man Foods (▷ 32)

Whole Foods Market
  (▷ 68)
Zabar's (▷ 97)

HOMEWARES

ABC Carpet and Home
  (▷ 45)
Crate & Barrel (▷ 85)
Michael C. Fina (▷ 68)
Pearl River Mart (▷ 32)

SHOES

Alife Rivington Club
  (▷ 32)
DSW and Filene's (▷ 45)
Kenneth Cole (▷ 97)
Manolo Blahnik (▷ 68)

SPORTS GOODS

Nike Town NY (▷ 68)
Patagonia (▷ 97)

STATIONERY

Kate's Paperie (▷ 32)

TOYS

FAO Schwarz (▷ 68)

New York by Night

As the sun sets over New York, the city becomes at once a sultry, romantic and mysterious place. Wander through Times Square as the glitzy electric billboards pop out from the dark sky. A stroll, run or bike ride along the pedestrian path on the banks of the Hudson River on the West Side offers a spectacular view of the sunset and the Jersey shore.

Nightlife

Clubs and restaurants come to life after dark. As young New Yorkers explore new frontiers in the city, the Meatpacking District—once known for drugs and prostitution—has become home to trendy bars and clubs. Celebrity sightings are common at Spice Market (✉ 403 W 13th Street ☎ 212/675-2322) and 5 Ninth (✉ 5 9th Avenue ☎ 212/929-9460). At the other end of the spectrum are biker bars like Hogs-n-Heiffers (✉ 859 Washington Street, at W 13th Street) and Fat Cat Billiards (✉ 75 Christopher Street nearby in West Village), friendly dives where the beer flows cheaply and the music blares loudly.

Take to the Water

Circle Line Cruises' evening boat rides around Manhattan are a relaxing way to see the world's most famous skyline. Board at Pier 83, at 42nd Street on the Hudson River (☎ 212/563-3200). Tour guides on board explain the legends of the city (www.circleline42.com).

FOR A LAUGH

Comedy clubs are a great way to sample New York's sense of humor. Venues such as Caroline's (✉ 1626 Broadway, at 50th Street ☎ 212/757–4100), Upright Citizens Brigade Theater (✉ 307 W 26th Street, between 8th and 9th ☎ 212/366–9176) and Stand Up NY (✉ 236 W 78th, at Broadway ☎ 212/595–0850) are popular. Gotham (✉ 208 W 23rd Street between 7th and 8th avenues ☎ 212/367–9000) has even been known to host surprise visits from Jerry Seinfeld.

Bright lights of Times Square and clubbers enjoying New York's nightlife

Eating Out

You can dine around the world in New York City. Some New Yorkers dine out every night, others save the top-class choices for special occasions. Dining trends change from season to season.

Plan Ahead
It's wise to make a reservation for dinner, especially on weekends. Indeed, top-class restaurants always require reservations. If you want a table at Jean-Georges, Le Bernardin, Per Se or similar, call well in advance. Sometimes it can be tough to get through even to the reservationists. Just keep trying. You may be able to eat at the bar in one of these fancy restaurants. In Midtown, luncheon reservations are also often essential. Very few places still require a jacket and tie at dinner so ask when making a reservation. In general, casual smart is the way to go.

Vegetarian Options
Many of the top-class dining rooms offer vegetarian menus, and even fast-food joints are offering more healthful options on their menus these days.

When to Go
Breakfast may be served all day at coffee shops and diners, but usual breakfast hours are from 7 to 11am. Lunch usually runs from 11.30am to 2.30pm and dinner from 5pm to 10 or 11pm. Many restaurants offer brunch on weekends.

TAXES, TIPPING AND FINANCIAL MATTERS
A sales tax of 8.375 percent will be added to your dining bill. The minimum tip (with good service) is 15 percent; many people double the tax for a 16.75 percent tip. Many restaurants offer prix-fixe menus, which are good value. In January and late June, a special promotion offers a three-course menu at reduced rates for lunch and dinner at numerous restaurants; this promotion is often extended so it's always worth checking if it's available.

Eating an ice cream; Costa Azzurra in Little Italy; hot dog; café at South Street Seaport; bagels

Restaurants by Cuisine

There are restaurants to suit all tastes and budgets in New York. On this page they are listed by cuisine. For a more detailed description of each restaurant, see New York by Area.

ASIAN

Jing Fong (▷ 34)
Nobu (▷ 34)
Osaka (▷ 108)
Sushi of Gari (▷ 88)

CASUAL

Barney Greengrass (▷ 100)
Boat Basin Café (▷ 100)
Bubby's (▷ 108)
Carmine's (▷ 100)
Jackson Hole (▷ 88)
Junior's (▷ 108)

CLASSIC

Le Bernardin (▷ 70)
Café des Artistes (▷ 100)
Café Boulud (▷ 88)
Chanterelle (▷ 34)
Daniel (▷ 88)
Del Posto (▷ 48)

Gramercy Tavern (▷ 48)

CLASSIC NY

'21' Club (▷ 70)
Boat House (▷ 88)
Four Seasons (▷ 70)
Katz's Deli (▷ 34)
Odeon (▷ 34)
Oyster Bar (▷ 70)
Peter Luger (▷ 108)
Serendipity 3 (▷ 88)
Tavern on the Green (▷ 88)

COMFORT FOOD

Schillers (▷ 34)
Spotted Pig (▷ 48)
Veselka (▷ 48)

CONTEMPORARY

Blue Ribbon (▷ 108)
Café Gray (▷ 70)

Gotham Bar and Grill (▷ 48)
Grocery (▷ 108)
Jean-Georges (▷ 100)
Lever House (▷ 70)
The Modern (▷ 70)
Per Se (▷ 70)
Thor (▷ 34)

EUROPEAN

Al di La (▷ 108)
Aix (▷ 100)
Bette (▷ 48)
Café Sabarsky (▷ 88)
Ouest (▷ 100)
Picholine (▷ 100)
Pintxos (▷ 34)
Sherwood Café (▷ 108)

MEXICAN

Mary Ann's (▷ 48)

If You Like...

However you'd like to spend your time in New York, these top suggestions should help you tailor your ideal visit. Each sight or listing has a fuller write-up in New York by Area.

STAR CHEFS

Jean Georges Vongerichten's Jean Georges restaurant (▷ 100) is the flagship of his ever-growing worldwide empire.
Daniel Boulud at Café Boulud will wow you (▷ 88). Don't forget the madeleines.
Good luck scoring a table at Per Se (▷ 70). Thomas Keller has been called the best chef in America. Often.
For fish, nobody beats Eric Ripert at Le Bernardin (▷ 70).

STAYING HIP

Trot over to Jeffrey New York (▷ 45) to refresh your wardrobe, or for vintage, Resurrection (▷ 32).
Get a taste of the LES at the Parkside Lounge (▷ 33).
Have a late supper at The Spotted Pig (▷ 48).
Bed down at 60 Thompson (▷ 114), the Gansevoort (▷ 114) or, if broke, Hotel QT (▷ 111).

*If you enjoy fine food, you w[ill]
love the choice and quality [to]
be found in New York*

TO PARTY TILL DAWN

O Bar is a scene, especially the garden in summer (▷ 46).
Go with the groove at the late-night jazz series Friday and Saturday from 12.30am at the Blue Note (▷ 46).
Blue Ribbon is at its busiest late (▷ 108).
NYC's best cheesecake at 3am? Junior's! (▷ 108).

Classic views of New York, from on high (above) and ground level, in the greenery of Central Park (right)

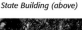

BIG AND BEAUTIFUL VIEWS

Harbor rooms at the Ritz-Carlton Battery Park (▷ 114) come complete with telescope.

Take in the lovely lake view from Central Park's Boat House (▷ 88)—unique in Manhattan.

Not everyone knows about the Iris and B. Gerald Cantor Roof Garden (▷ 86) at the Met.

If you're not staying at Beekman Tower (▷ 112), visit the 26th-floor restaurant/bar.

Top of the Rock (▷ 62) rivals the Empire State Building (▷ 54–55) for the best view in town.

BRINGING THE KIDS

FAO Schwarz (▷ 68) is more than a store—especially since the renovation.

They won't believe the five-story indoor ferris wheel at Toys R Us, Times Square (▷ 63).

Bloomingdale's (top); view from the Empire State Building (above)

You can never go wrong with a zoo. Bronx Zoo is vast (▷ 106); the one in Central Park (▷ 74–75) won't take all day.

Take them to Serendipity 3 (▷ 88) for frozen hot chocolate.

Get tickets for The New Victory Theater (▷ 69).

CLASSIC NYC

See the ceiling, covered in toy trucks at the clubby 21 Club (▷ 70).

Bergdorfs, Saks and Bloomies are classic department stores with different personalities (▷ 68, 85).

The Chrysler Building (▷ 52–53) is New York's favorite skyscraper and an art deco masterpiece.

See how the other half lived at the Frick (▷ 77) and Cooper-Hewitt (▷ 76).

Entrance to the Bronx Zoo (above middle); the famous spire of the Chrysler Building towers above the city (left)

SPORTING PURSUITS

Hope you're here in baseball season (April to September; post-season to October). Yankee Stadium (▷ 107) is a must. Or catch the Mets at Shea.

Madison Square Garden has it all (▷ 65, 69): basketball (the Knicks), boxing, tennis, track and field…

There's a game of something in progress in Central Park (▷ 74–75) all summer long. If it's winter, you can skate at Wollman Rink.

Shop for outdoor sports gear at Patagonia (▷ 97).

A LAUGH

Caroline Hirsch broke Jerry Seinfeld, Tim Allen and Rosie O'Donnell. Twenty-something years on her club, Caroline's (▷ 69), still rocks.

A nongrungy stand-up venue: Gotham Comedy Club (▷ 46).

Score free tickets for a taping of Conan O'Brien or the *Daily Show* with Jon Stewart (▷ 62).

Look for whimsical artworks at MoMA (▷ 60) or the New Museum of Contemporary Art (▷ 29).

EATING WHERE IT'S AT

Thor is a showcase for people as well as Kurt Gutenbrunner's food (▷ 34).

To spot models, try Schiller's (▷ 34) late.

Amy Sacco runs the best nightclubs, and now a restaurant, too. Head for Bette (▷ 48).

All Mario Batali's places are hot spots; his fanciest by far is Del Posto (▷ 48).

Taste a little of the Brooklyn scene at Sherwood Café (▷ 108).

American sports and entertainment can be enjoyed year-round

Take time to dine out, the choice of good city restaurants is vast (right)

New York by Area

特價 $48.50/LB 碼
特宗谷元貝碎
大宗谷元貝碎

$11.50

$50

$36

日本宗
江瑤？

The cradle of New York, Lower Manhattan has bags of history—new citizens in the 19th century first landed here—as well as the financial district, the historic seaport district and iconic Statue of Liberty.

Around Lower Manhattan

18

19

20

21

22

23

C   **D**   **E**

Clarkson   Street

HOUSTON   Houston   VARICK
Street   Street

HUDSON STREET   King   Charlton   STREET   Prince   Street   Mulberry   **St Patrick's**
    Old Cathedral
WEST   Greenwich   Charlton   AVENUE OF THE AMERICAS (6TH AVENUE)   Prince   Street   **Singer**   Spring   Street   Mott   Street
    Building
    Spring   Street   Spring   Street
    Spring   Vandam   Sullivan   West Broadway   Wooster Street   Greene Street   Crosby   Kenmare   Street
    Street   Spring   Street   **SOHO**   **Haughwout**   **Building**   **LITTLE ITALY**
    Dominick   Broome   Street   **Children's**   Broome   Street
    New York City Fire   Street   Street   **Museum**   Broome   Street
    Department Museum   Renwick   Watts   Grand   **of the Arts**
    Street   Spring   Street   Thompson St   Grand   Street   Howard   street   Heste
    Watts   Mercer Street
HOLLAND TUNNEL   Canal   Street   **Canal**   Greene Street   Broadway   Street
    WEST   CANAL   Canal   Street   **Street**   Mott Street
    STREET   Watts   Street   Park   Canal   Street   Canal
    Desbrosses   Street   **Canal**   Street   Street   Canal   Street
    Vestry   Street   **Street**   Wooster Street   Museum of Chinese
    LAIGHT STREET   Lispenard   **LOWER MANHATTAN**   in the Americas
    Hubert   HUDSON STREET   White   Bayard   white Street
    Beach St   Walker   Street   **Columbus**
    Ericsson   **Place**   West Broadway   White   Street   **Park**
    Franklin   Franklin   Place   CENTRE STREET
    North Moore   **Street**   Franklin   Street   Hogan
    Beach St   LAFAYETTE STREET   Place   PARK RO
    Harrison   Leonard   Street   Thomas Paine
    TRIBECA   Worth   Park   Foley
    Street   Street   Square
    Harrison   Thomas   Street   Pearl   Street
    Duane   Street   US   Street
Washington   Greenwich Street   Duane   **Courthouse**   Cardinal   Street
Market Park   Reade St   **Chambers**   Reade   Street   Cardinal Hayes
    CHAMBERS   **Street**   City   Chambers   **Chambers**   Pl
    Reade   Street   Hall   **Street**   **Brooklyn Bridge –**
Warren   **Chambers**   Warren   City   **City Hall**
Street   **Street**   Warren   Street   Hall Park   **City Hall**   BROOKLY
Park   Murray   Street   **BROADWAY**
Place West   Murray   Murray   Street   Park Row   Spruce   Spruce St
    BARCLAY   Park   **Woolworth**   Beekman   Street
Barclay   Vesey   Street   Place   **Building**   Ann   Street
Street   **VESEY STREET**   CHURCH STREET   Park   **Broadway–**   Dutch   Fulton
    Place   + **Church of**   **Nassau St**   Street
    St Paul's Chapel   **St Peter**   Ann   Fulton   Street
    World Trade   Fulton St   Fulton   Fulton
    Center   Dey   **Street**   John   Street
BATTERY   **Ground**   Cortlandt   street   **American**
PARK CITY   **Zero**   Cortlandt   John   **Numismatic**
    Cortlandt   **MAIDEN LANE**   **Society**   Platt
WEST STREET   Liberty   Street   **Federal Reserve**   Liberty   Street   Gold   John   Fletche
    Liberty   Street   **Bank**   William
    Cedar   Street   MAIDEN   LAN
    Albany   Greenwich Street   **Trinity**   Pine   **Federal Hall**   **Museum of America**
    Street   **Church** +   Wall   **National**   **Financial History**
    Rector   Rector   Street   Wall   **Memorial**   **Wall** Street
    Place   **Street**   Street   Nassau Street   Broad   WILLIAM STREET
    Rector   **New York**   Wall   Street   **WALL**
    Place   **Stock Exchange**   BROADWAY   Street   **STREET**
    West Thames   Exchange   Street   Broad   OLD SLIP
    Street   BROAD STREET   Exchange   Alv   Street   Place   **New York**
    Morris   **City Police**
    2nd Place   Morris   Street   Beaver   stone Street   **Museum**
    Battery   **Bowling**   Beaver   SOUTH STREET
    GREENWICH STREET   **Green**   Fraunces Tavern
    Battery   **Museum**   Gouverne
    Museum of   Place   **Bowling**   Whitehall   Vietnam Veterans
    Jewish Heritage   Battery   **Green**   Street   Plaza
    Robert   Place   Pearl   Water Street
    F Wagner   STATE STREET   **Rectory of the Shrine**
    Jr Park   **Battery**   **of Elizabeth Ann Seton**
    Park   PETER MINUIT
    Castle   PLAZA
    Clinton   South
    Admiral George   Ferry
    Dewey Promenade   HIGHWAY 9A   Staten Island   **Ellis Island**
    BROOKLYN BATTERY TUNNEL   Ferry Terminal   **& Statue**
    of Liberty

Hudson

0 ——— 300 m
0 ——— 250 yds

New Museum of Contemporary Art

Rivington Street

DELANCEY
STREET

Delancey
Street

Lower East Side Tenement Museum

Essex
Street

LOWER EAST SIDE

Grand
Street

Grand
Street

Hester
Street

Canal
Street

Seward
Park

Broome
Street

Grand
Street

WILLIAMSBURG   BRIDGE   APPROACH

Rivington Street

Baruch Drive

Broome
Street

East
Broadway

Division
Street

East
Broadway

Jefferson St.

CHINATOWN

Division
Street

Monroe st.

Cherry

Rutgers
Park

Mills
Road

the   Finest

FRANKLIN DELANO ROOSEVELT DRIVE

MANHATTAN   BRIDGE

East

BRIDGE

SOUTH STREET

BROOKLYN   BRIDGE

Fulton Street Market

South Street Seaport

F   G   H

Chinatown

Streetlife in Chinatown
(left and below)

THE BASICS

F20

✉ Roughly delineated by Worth Street/East Broadway, the Bowery, Grand Street, Centre Street

🍴 Numerous (some close around 10pm)

🚇 J, M, N, Q, R, W, Z, 6, A, C, E, 1, Canal Street; B, D Grand Street

🚌 M1, B51

♿ Poor

❓ General tours

☎ 212/465-3331; NYC Discovery Tours

HIGHLIGHTS

● Buddhist temple (✉ 64B Mott Street)
● Chinatown History Museum (✉ 70 Mulberry Street)
● Pearl River Mart (✉ 477 Broadway, ▷ 32)
● Doyers Street: once the "Bloody Angle"
● Columbus Park (✉ Bayard/Baxter streets)

New York's Chinatown has swallowed nearly all of Little Italy and has spread over a great deal of the Lower East Side. Wander here and you're humbled by the sight of a lifestyle that thrives.

Going west Chinese people first came to New York in the late 19th century, looking to work for a while, make some money and return home. But, by 1880 or so, some 10,000 men—mostly Cantonese railroad workers decamped from California—had been stranded between Canal, Worth and Baxter streets. Tongs (bands of secret mafia-like operations) were formed, and still keep order over some 150,000 or more Chinese, Taiwanese, Vietnamese, Burmese and Singaporeans. New York, incidentally, has two more Chinatowns: in Flushing (Queens) and 8th Avenue, Brooklyn, with a further 150,000 or more inhabitants, but Manhattan's is the world's largest.

A closed world Although you may happily wander its colorful streets, you will never penetrate Chinatown. Many of its denizens never learn English and never leave its environs. The 600 factories and 350 restaurants keep them in work; then there are the tea shops, mah-jongg parlors, herbalists, and the highest bank-to-citizen ratio in New York, in which Chinese stash their wages (normally not more than $10,000–$20,000 a year) to save for the "eight bigs" (car, TV, DVD player, fridge, camera, phone, washing machine and furniture), to send home, or eventually to invest in a business of their own.

TOP 25

Ellis Island at night
(below); a Circle Line
ferry passing Ellis
Island (right)

Ellis Island

TOP 25

This museum offers a taste of how the huddled masses of new immigrants were not allowed to go free until they'd been herded through these halls, weighed, measured and rubber stamped.

Half of all America It was the poor who docked at Ellis Island after sometimes grueling voyages in steerage, since first-class passage included permission to decant straight into Manhattan. Annie Moore, aged 15 and the first immigrant to disembark here, arrived in 1892, followed by 16 million immigrants over the next 40 years, including such then-fledgling Americans as Irving Berlin and Frank Capra. Half the population of the United States can trace their roots to an Ellis Island immigrant.

Island of Tears The exhibition in the main building conveys the indignities, frustrations and fears of the arrivals. (As you arrive, collect your free ticket for the half-hour film, *Island of Hope/Island of Tears*, or you'll miss it.) You are guided around more or less the same route new arrivals took: from the Baggage Room, where they had to abandon all they owned; onward to the large Registry Room, now bare of furniture; and through the inspection chambers where medical, mental and political status were ascertained. The Oral History Studio brings it all to life as immigrants recount their experience—especially moving when coupled with the poignant items in the "Treasures from Home" exhibit. This is a demanding few hours' sightseeing. Wear sensible shoes and bring lunch.

THE BASICS

www.ellisisland.com
⊞ Off map at E23
✉ Ellis Island
☎ 212/363–3200
⊙ Daily 9.30–5, closed 25 Dec
🍴 Café
🚇 4, 5 Bowling Green, then take ferry
🚌 M1, M6, M15, then take the ferry
⛴ Ferry departs Battery Park South Ferry every 30 mins. Ferry information
☎ 212/269–5755
♿ Good
💵 Museum free; ferry expensive
❓ Audio tours available

HIGHLIGHTS

● Wall of Honor
● Treasures from Home
● Oral History Studio
● Dormitory
● Augustus Sherman's photos
● View of Lower Manhattan

Statue of Liberty

HIGHLIGHTS

- View from the pedestal
- Statue of Liberty Museum
- Fort Wood, the star-shape pedestal base
- Her new centenary flame

TIP

- A visit to the Statue of Liberty can be combined with a trip to Ellis Island since most ferries stop at both islands.

The green lady, symbol of the American dream of freedom, takes your breath away, however many times you've seen her photograph—and despite her surprisingly modest stature.

How she grew In the late 1860s, sculptor Frédéric-Auguste Bartholdi dreamed of placing a monument to freedom in a prominent location. His dream merged with the French historian Edouard-René de Laboulaye's idea of presenting the American people with a statue that celebrated freedom and the two nations' friendship. Part of the idea was to shame the repressive French government, but, apparently, New Yorkers took their freedom for granted: It was only after Joseph Pulitzer promised to print the name of every donor in his newspaper, the *New York World*, that

Clockwise from left: tourists posing at the base of the Statue of Liberty; Liberty seen on her island; detail of one of the most famous statues in the world; a coin-operated lookout point for viewing the Statue of Liberty

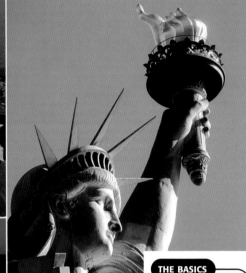

the city's citizens coughed up the funds to build the pedestal. Liberty was unveiled by President Grover Cleveland on October 28, 1886.

Mother of exiles Emma Lazarus' stirring poem, *The New Colossus*, is engraved on the pedestal, while the tablet reads: July IV MDCCLXXVI—the date of the Declaration of Independence. Beneath her size 107 feet, she tramples the shackles of tyranny, and her seven-pointed crown beams liberty to the seven continents and the seven seas.

What is she made of? Gustave Eiffel practiced for his later work by designing the 1,700-bar iron and steel structure that supports her. She weighs 225 tons, is 151ft (46m) tall, has an 8ft (2m) index finger and a skin of 300 copper plates. The torch tip towers 305ft (93m) above sea level.

THE BASICS

www.nps.gov/stli
✚ Off map at E23
✉ Liberty Island
☎ 212/363-3200
🕐 Daily 9.30–5; extended hours in peak season. A limited number of daily tickets to tour the monument may be reserved in advance from ferry office or by phone
🍴 Cafeteria
Ⓜ 4, 5 Bowling Green, then take ferry
🚌 M1, M6, M15 South Ferry, then take ferry
⛴ Ferry departs Battery Park South Ferry (AF19). Ferry information
☎ 212/269–5755
♿ Poor
💲 Free; ferry expensive

South Street Seaport

TOP 25

THE BASICS

www.southstseaport.org

✚ F21

✉ Visitor center: 12 Fulton Street. Tickets also from Pier 16

☎ 212/748–8600

🕓 Most shops Mon–Sat 10–9, Sun 11–8; Museum: Apr–Oct Tue–Sun 10–6; Nov–Mar Fri–Sun 10–5, ships 12–5. Also Schermerhorn Row galleries only on Mon 10–5. Closed Dec 25 and Jan 1

🍽 Numerous

🚇 2, 3, 4, 5, J, M, Z Fulton Street; A, C Broadway-Nassau Street

🚌 M15 Pearl/Fulton Street

♿ Poor

💲 Moderate

HIGHLIGHTS

● View of Brooklyn Heights
● Richard Haas' Brooklyn Bridge mural
● The historic buildings of Schermerhorn Row
● Boarding *Andrew Fletcher*
● Titanic Memorial
● Chandlery
● Fulton Market (especially the bakeries)

This reconstructed historic maritime district, with its cobbled streets, is a tourist trap. However, when you stroll the boardwalk on a summer's night, with the moon over the East River, you are very glad to be a tourist.

Pier, cruise, shop, eat The seaside/cruise-ship atmosphere is what's fun at the Pier 17 Pavilion, which juts 400ft (122m) into the East River, overlooking Brooklyn Heights. It's a mall, with chain stores, bad restaurants and a food court, but also three stories of charming wooden decks. The adjoining piers, 16 and 15, harbor a number of historic vessels with picturesque arrangements of rigging, as well as the replica side-wheeler *Andrew Fletcher* and the 1885 schooner *Pioneer*, which give harbor cruises. Your cash is courted by many stores, housed in the 1812 Federal-style warehouses of Schermerhorn Row—Manhattan's oldest block—and around Water, Front and Fulton streets, and by the cafés in the old Fulton Market.

Many museums The Seaport Museum Visitors' Center acts as clearing house for all the small-scale exhibitions here. One ticket admits you to the second-biggest sailing ship ever built, the *Peking*; the floating lighthouse, Ambrose; the Children's Center; the Seaport Museum Gallery; a re-creation of a 19th-century printer's shop; various walking tours (including "Ship Restoration" and "Back Streets"—worthwhile if you have the time) and more.

More to See

BATTERY PARK

This refuge for workers in the Financial District was named for the cannon sited here to defend the fledgling city against British attack. Buy tickets for the Statue of Liberty at Castle Clinton.

E23 ✉ Tip of Manhattan 🚇 1, South Ferry; 4, 5 Bowling Green

CHILDREN'S MUSEUM OF THE ARTS

Highlights include the Monet Ballpond, Architects Alley and the Wonder Theater.

E18/19 ✉ 182 Lafayette Street ☎ 212/274-0986 🕐 Wed, Fri–Sun 12–5, Thu 12–6 🚇 6 Spring Street ✋ Moderate (adult), free (child)

CITY HALL

French Renaissance-style facade and elegant Georgian interior—see it by visiting the Governor's Room, with a small furniture museum.

E20 ✉ Broadway/Murray Street ☎ 212/788-3000 🕐 Mon–Fri 10–3.30 🚇 2, 3 Park Place; 4, 5, 6 Brooklyn Bridge-City Hall; N, R City Hall ✋ Free

GROUND ZERO

The exact nature of the building that will replace the Twin Towers, destroyed by terrorists on 9/11 2001, remains undecided at the time of writing, but completion is estimated at 2011.

D21 ✉ Church to West streets, Liberty to Vesey streets 🚇 E World Trade Center

LOWER EAST SIDE TENEMENT MUSEUM

This reconstruction of life in an 1863 tenement block is a must for history buffs. Intriguing tours and talks.

G18 ✉ 108 Orchard Street ☎ 212/431-0233 🕐 Tue–Fri 1–4, Sat–Sun 11–4.30 🚇 F, J, M, Z Delancey Street; B, D, Q Grand Street ✋ Expensive

NEW MUSEUM OF CONTEMPORARY ART

The striking white, modern building that houses this cutting-edge museum is the talk of the Lower East Side.

F18 ✉ 235 Bowery/Prince Street ☎ 212/219-1222 🕐 Wed–Sun 12–6, Thu–Fri 12–10 🚇 N, R Prince Street ✋ Expensive

A poignant tribute at Ground Zero

World Trade Center Globe Statue Memorial, Battery Park

NEW YORK CITY POLICE MUSEUM

A small museum with a wealth of cops and robbers material including handguns, uniforms and shields. You can visit a prison cell and learn about forensics. The NYPD Hall of Heroes includes a memorial to the policemen and women who died on 9/11 2001.

✚ F22 ✉ 100 Old Slip ☎ 212/480–3100 🕙 Mon–Sat 10–5 🚇 2, 3 Wall Street ✋ Donation suggested, moderate

NEW YORK STOCK EXCHANGE

The neoclassical facade dates only from 1903. The Stock Exchange is not currently open for visits or tours. Telephone for up-to-date information.

✚ E22 ✉ 20 Broad Street ☎ 212/656–3000 🚇 2, 3, 4, 5 Wall Street; J, M, Z Broad Street

ST. PATRICK'S OLD CATHEDRAL

New York's first Roman Catholic cathedral opened in 1815. At that time, the area was settled by Irish immigrants. The original structure was destroyed in a fire in 1866, but enlarged and rebuilt by 1868. When the new St. Pat's (▷ 66) was built in 1879, the cathedral became a parish church.

✚ F18 ✉ 263 Mulberry Street ☎ 212/226-8075 (call for times) 🚇 N R, Q Prince Street

SINGER BUILDING AND HAUGHWOUT BUILDING

Two of the best ambassadors for the SoHo Cast Iron Historic District—the 26 blocks of skyscraper forerunners, now galleries and upscale boutiques. The Haughwout had the first Otis steam elevator.

✚ E18 ✉ Singer: 561 Broadway. Haughwout: 488 Broadway 🚇 N, R Prince Street; F, B, D Broadway-Lafayette Street

WOOLWORTH BUILDING

The world's tallest until the Chrysler, Cass Gilbert's Gothic beauty has NYC's richest lobby—with witty bas reliefs of Gilbert and tycoon F. W. Woolworth. It now contains condos and is unfortunately closed to the public.

✚ E21 ✉ 233 Broadway 🚇 2, 3 Park Place; N, R City Hall

Woolworth Building

Interior of St. Patrick's Old Cathedral

Lower Manhattan to Downtown

A stroll through the highlights of downtown.

DISTANCE: 2 miles (3km) **ALLOW:** 40 minutes

START

CHURCH STREET
✛ E21 Ⓜ Park Place 2, 3

END

GREENWICH VILLAGE (▷ 40)
✛ C17 Ⓜ W 4th Street A, B, C, D, F, V

1 Walk east on Barclay Street, turn left onto Broadway and look to your left for the Woolworth Building. At City Hall Park continue along Broadway, where City Hall comes into view on your right.

2 Walk east through the park and catch a vista of Brooklyn Bridge. Continue north up Centre Street to Cass Gilbert's US Courthouse on Foley Square.

3 The neoclassical New York County Courthouse is past Pearl Street on the right, and then, past Hogan Place, the Criminal Courts (The Tombs).

4 Another block, and here's Canal Street. Go east to Mulberry Street. Continue north through Little Italy and veer west on Prince Street to the Cast Iron Historic District of SoHo.

8 Keep heading west to expore the Village further.

7 Fifth Avenue starts at the north side. Look at gated Washington Square Mews (first right), turn left on W 8th Street (see MacDougal Alley, first left) to Avenue of the Americas (6th Avenue).

6 Take any route west through the streets of SoHo, heading north across Houston Street anywhere from Mercer to MacDougal; now you're in Greenwich Village. Three blocks north, you reach Washington Square, the center of New York University.

5 Look at the Singer Building opposite as you cross Broadway.

Shopping

ABERCROMBIE & FITCH

Teens and college grads are the core customers at this temple to slouchy American style, famous for its rather racy Bruce Weber-shot catalogs. The clothes, though, are good for anyone's weekends and the prices are gentle. There are men's and women's lines.

➕ F21 ✉ 199 Water Street/Fulton Street
☎ 212/809-9000 🚇 2, 3, 4, 5, A, C, J, M, Z Fulton Street-Broadway-Nassau

ALIFE RIVINGTON CLUB

Here behind an unmarked door, trainers are high fashion, with all the latest footwear from American, European and Japanese lines. Great colors, limited editions.

➕ G18 ✉ 158 Rivington Street, between Clinton and Suffolk streets ☎ 212/375-8128 🚇 F, J, M, Z Delancey Street/Essex Street

BROOKS BROTHERS

Home of the preppy, Brooks Brothers also caters to anyone, male or female (though the men's department is far better) who wants to look pulled together. Their basics, like boxer shorts and white dress shirts, are exceptional.

➕ E21 ✉ 1 Church Street/Liberty Plaza
☎ 212/267-2400 🚇 4, 5 Fulton Street

CENTURY 21

Practically a cult, especially in the European designer area.

➕ E21 ✉ 22 Cortlandt Street ☎ 212/227-9092
🚇 4, 5 Fulton Street

GOURMET GARAGE

The place to find yellow cherry tomatoes, dried cherries, fresh clams, truffle butter, smoked duck, gelati, you-name-it.

➕ E18 ✉ 435 Broome Street/Mercer Street
☎ 212/941-5850 🚇 N, R Prince Street

INA

Showroom samples and barely worn designer duds. The prices are high, but fair; there's a men's version round the corner.

➕ D18 ✉ 101 Thompson Street ☎ 212/941-4757
🚇 N, R Prince Street

PEARL RIVER MART

Shop here for chrome lunch pails with clip-on lids; embroidered silk pajamas and Suzy Wong dresses; bamboo fans and porcelain rice bowls—all the things, in fact, you can get in the smaller Chinatown emporia, but collected under one roof. The food department sells an eclectic range. The prices are very, very low.

➕ E18 ✉ 477 Broadway (Broome Street) ☎ 212/431-4770 🚇 N, R Canal Street

KAM MAN FOODS

This large Chinese food store overflows with exotic products, from live fish and edible bird's nests to ginseng priced at hundreds of dollars. It also sells inexpensive Asian cookware.

➕ F19 ✉ 200 Canal Street/Mott Street ☎ 212/571-0330
🚇 J, M, Z Canal Street

KATE'S PAPERIE

The beautiful handmade stationery is overwhelming at this SoHo boutique.

➕ E18 ✉ 72 Spring Street between Crosby and Lafayette streets ☎ 212/941-9816
🚇 6 Spring Street

THE MYSTERIOUS BOOKSHOP

A must for mystery lovers. Staff will lead you to new discoveries alongside famous writers from Raymond Chandler to Patricia Highsmith. Also rare volumes and first editions.

➕ E20 ✉ 58 Warren Street/Church Street
☎ 212/587-1011 🚇 1, 2, 3, A, C, E Chambers Street

RESURRECTION

A haul of pricey but perfect vintage, with an emphasis on collectible labels: Pucci, Halston, Courrèges, Dior et al. The owners also offer their own line of skirts and tops.

➕ F18 ✉ 217 Mott Street between Spring and Prince streets ☎ 212/625-1374
🚇 6 Spring Street

Entertainment and Nightlife

ARLENE'S GROCERY

One of the best rock clubs in the city, where hot new bands make their name.

➕ G18 ✉ 95 Stanton Street, between Ludlow and Orchard streets ☎ 212/995-1652 🚇 F, V 2nd Avenue

BARRAMUNDI

Woodsy decor, a neighborhood crowd, Aussie beers and a new flavor of infused vodka every week are among the draws at this Lower East Side hangout.

➕ G18 ✉ 67 Clinton Street near Rivington Street ☎ 212/529-6900 🚇 F, J, M, Z Delancey Street-Essex Street

BOWERY BALLROOM

This venue lets the alternative musicians spread out a bit. It is indeed like a ballroom, with a proscenium arch stage.

➕ F18 ✉ 6 Delancey Street/ Bowery ☎ 212/533-2111 🚇 J, M Bowery, 6 Spring Street

BRIDGE CAFÉ

This loveable place has been serving continuously since 1794—yes it's one of the oldest taverns in town. The bar is a lovely place to end an evening after a stroll by the water.

➕ F21 ✉ 279 Water Street/Dover Street ☎ 212/227-3344 🚇 4, 5, 6 Brooklyn Bridge-City Hall

THE KNITTING FACTORY

The Main Space, the KnitActive Sound Stage, the Old Office and the Tap Bar are the four performance rooms at the leading venue for new music.

➕ E20 ✉ 74 Leonard Street (Church Street/Broadway) ☎ 212/219-3132 🚇 1 Franklin Street

MAKOR

A wide variety of concerts, from rap to blues to world music, films and other events are held at this new venue of the Jewish community center.

➕ D19 ✉ 200 Hudson Street between Vestry and Desbrosses streets ☎ 212/601-1000 🚇 1, A, C, E Canal Street

PARKSIDE LOUNGE

A multipurpose venue that hosts live music, stand-ups and karaoke, and people having a beer. It's open until 4am. An unpretentious minimally art-directed place to sample the Lower East Side buzz.

➕ G17 ✉ 317 E Houston Street/Attorney Avenue ☎ 212/673-6270 🚇 F, V 2nd Avenue

RISE

The cocktail area of the Ritz-Carlton is not your typical hotel bar.

➕ D23 ✉ 2 West Street/ Battery Place, 14th floor ☎ 917/790-2626 🚇 4, 5 Bowling Green

S.O.B.'S

The Latin beat keeps you dancing at this tropically themed nightclub ("Sounds of Brazil"). Also African, reggae and other island music.

➕ D18 ✉ 204 Varick Street ☎ 212/243-4940 🚇 1 Houston Street

COCKTAIL CULTURE

Cocktail culture is alive and well in the Big Apple. The Martini craze is here to stay—many lounges and bars offer long menus of creative concoctions. Elegant glassware is crucial. Atmospheres range from urban chic to clubby lounge to pubs. Neighborhood pubs, with more emphasis on beer and bourbon, are favorite watering holes. Or, instead of alcohol, visit one of New York's coffee bars.

KEEPING UP

One of New York's favorite pastimes is keeping up with what's on. Look for extensive weekly listings in the magazines *New York, Time Out New York* and *New Yorker*, or the Friday and Sunday editions of the *New York Times*. You can also pick up free copies of the *Village Voice* and *New York Press* newspapers in storefronts and vestibules around town. The monthly listings in *Paper* magazine have a decidedly downtown focus.

Restaurants

PRICES

Prices are approximate, based on a 3-course meal for one person.
$$$ over $60
$$ $40–$60
$ under $40

CHANTERELLE ($$$)

Serene restaurant on a quiet Tribeca corner. Billowy curtains, flower arrangements and elegant tables provide the perfect backdrop for a romantic evening. The seafood sausage is a dream.
✚ D20 ✉ 2 Harrison Street/Hudson Street ☎ 212/966-6960 🕐 Closed Sun, Mon lunch 🚇 1 Franklin Street

JING FONG ($)

An unmissable dim sum experience: trolleys laden with everything from steamed pork buns to stewed chicken feet whizz through an enormous room—hail them before the best bits go.
✚ F19 ✉ 20 Elizabeth Street/Bayard and Canal streets ☎ 212/ 964-5256 🕐 Go before 3pm 🚇 6, N, R Canal Street

KATZ'S DELI ($)

The site of the hilarious climactic scene in *When Harry Met Sally* is the last remaining deli in what was a thriving Jewish neighborhood. Opened in 1888, it upholds traditions: nondescript surroundings and knishes and pastrami sandwiches.

✚ G17 ✉ 205 E Houston Street/Ludlow Street ☎ 212/254-2246 🚇 F, V Lower East Side-2nd Avenue

NOBU ($$$)

It is difficult to get a reservation at this Japanese shrine but you'll be rewarded by the hauntingly delicious food. The dining room is a modern Japanese fantasy with lots of bamboo. Choose from baby abalone, live scallops, or sashimi drizzled with garlic and ginger-infused olive oil.
✚ D19 ✉ 105 Hudson Street/Franklin Street ☎ 212/219-0500 🕐 Closed Sat, Sun lunch 🚇 1 Franklin Street

PINTXOS ($–$$)

Tapas lovers must try the Basque version of these artful little plates, ranging

ODEON ($$)

After celebrating its quarter-century in 2005 with all the 80s faces that made it the first hot spot of the *Bright Lights Big City* age, this art deco-style restaurant still outdoes half the new boîtes in town. Its tiled floors, dim lighting, happy bar area and open-most-hours welcome are some reasons why—that and the always-reliable nouvelle-American cooking.
✉ 145 West Broadway/Thomas Street ☎ 212/233-0507 🚇 A, C Chambers Street

from stuffed mussels and Basque anchovies to white asparagus or spicy chorizo. Have them as a starter before the meat and fish entrees or as a meal in themselves with regional wines. Small, cozy atmosphere.
✚ C18 ✉ 510 Greenwich Street between Canal and Spring streets ☎ 212/343-9923 🕐 Closed Sun 🚇 C, E Spring Street

SCHILLERS ($–$$)

www.schillersny.com
The latest hit from the man who brought faux-France to Manhattan (Balthazar, Pastis) veers toward the Mitteleuropa-deli model. It's quite a scene, though off-hours tend to be peaceful.
✚ G18 ✉ 131 Rivington Street/Norfolk Street ☎ 212/260-4555 🚇 F, V Delancey Street-2nd Avenue

THOR ($$$)

The name is an acronym for the high-design hotel that houses it. As if to match the fabulous Marcel Wanders design, Austrian chef Kurt Gutenbrunner waxes more creative here than at his three other NY places: butter-poached lobster with cherries or white tomato mousse are the kind of dishes on the small-plate menu.
✚ G18 ✉ The Hotel on Rivington, 107 Rivington Street/Essex Street ☎ 212/796-8040 🚇 F, V Delancey-2nd Avenue

Downtown

Below 14th Street find the East Village and SoHo where everything from high-fashion stores and ethnic restaurants to bohemian bars and bijou theaters are open (almost) all hours.

13

10TH AVENUE

West 29th Street
West 28th Street
28th Street
West 27th Street

Chelsea Park

West 26th Street
West 25th Street

14

Chelsea Art Galleries

West 24th Street
23rd Street

10TH AVENUE
9TH AVENUE

West 23rd Street
23rd Street

West 22nd Street
West 21st Street

CHELSEA

West 20th Street

West 19th Street
West 18th Street
18th Street

8TH AVENUE
7TH AVENUE

West 17th Street

15

West 16th Street
West 15th Street
14th Street

11TH AVENUE

WEST 14TH STREET
8th Avenue
14th Street

West 13th Street

Washington Street

Greenwich

16

Bloomfield Street

Meatpacking District

Gansevoort Street

Horatio Street

Jane Street

Bethune Street

West Street

8TH AVENUE

Bank Street

Waverly

Jefferson Market Library

4th Street

Perry Street

Charles Street

West 12th Street
West 11th Street
West 10th Street
West 9th Street
West 8th Street

AVENUE OF THE AMERICAS (6TH AVENUE)

GREENWICH VILLAGE

Christopher Street - Sheridan Square

McNulty's Rare Teas and Choice Coffee Shop

Church of St. Luke-in-the-Fields

17

Hudson

WEST STREET
West State Service Road

Perry Street
Charles Lane
Charles Street
10th Street
Christopher Street
Barrow Street
Morton Street

Bedford Street
Commerce Street

Hudson Street

Leroy Street

Clarkson Street

J J Walker Park

Carmine Street
Downing Street

House of Oldies Rare Records

WEST HOUSTON STREET

0   300 m
0   250 yds

B   C   D

East Village

HIGHLIGHTS

● Sidewalk artists and book stalls
● Polish-Ukrainian restaurant, Veselka (▷ 48)

TIP

● For a calm break, head to Tompkins Square Park, bordered by avenues A and B, between 7th and 10th streets. Once the very definition of "needle park," it couldn't be nicer now, with fresh plantings and children frolicking on the lawns.

Once for those priced out of Greenwich Village, East Village is now expensive bohemia and what used to be the edgiest "nabe" in town is now a youthful playground of restaurants and boutiques with a smattering of historic sights.

Early days The area was settled by Dutch, Irish, German, Jewish and Ukrainian immigrants between 1800 and 1900. By 1830, the Vanderbilts, Astors and Delanos were among those who lived in grand houses on Lafayette Street.

Notable buildings Cooper Union, founded by engineer Peter Cooper and built by 1859, is a designated landmark and it was here that Abraham Lincoln made his famous anti-slavery

Clockwise from top left: typical East Village buildings; two carved lions at the entrance to the church of St. Marks in the Bowery; a colorful delivery vehicle; Astor Place; walking the streets; a decorated building

speech. West of St Mark's Square is the Gothic Revival Grace Church, built in 1846 by James Renwick Jr. Renwick was also responsible for the Federal-style Stuyvesant-Fish House, built in 1803 for Peter Stuyvesant who gave it as a wedding present to his daughter and Nicholas Fish. The Ukrainian Museum is an introduction to the cultural heritage of the Ukrainians who settled here. The displays include decorated Easter eggs, ritual cloths, costumes and a lot more.

Literary appeal A haunt of the Beat poets in the 1960s, East Village attracted Allen Ginsberg, Andy Warhol, Timothy Leary and many radicals. Today the area has its artists and literary types, as well as holding a great appeal to visitors. The range of budget ethnic restaurants and smart eateries offers plenty of choice for lunch.

THE BASICS

➕ F16; east of Bowery and south of 14th Street
🚇 F, V Lower East Side-2nd Avenue; 6 Astor Place

Ukrainian Museum
www.ukrainianmuseum.org
➕ F17
✉ 222 E 6th Street/2nd–3rd avenues
☎ 212/228-0110
🕐 Wed–Sun 11.30–5
♿ Moderate

39

Greenwich Village

The Row (left); Washington Arch (middle); Jefferson Market Library (below)

THE BASICS

+ C17
✉ East–west from Broadway to Hudson Street; north–south from 14th Street to Houston Street
🍴 Numerous
🚇 A, B, C, D, E, F, W 4th Street-Washington Square; 1 Christopher Street-Sheridan Square
🚌 M10
🚉 PATH Christopher Street
♿ Poor

HIGHLIGHTS

● Cafés and jazz clubs
● Washington Square Park
● NYC's narrowest house (75 Bedford Street)
● West (of Hudson Street) Village
● Halloween Parade
● Jefferson Market Library
● Citarella and Jefferson Market (food stores)
● Minetta Lane

This sugar-sweet, picturesque, human-scale neighborhood of brownstones and trees is one of the romantic images of Manhattan, familiar from sitcoms and movies. Its dense streets are rewarding to wander and you can take a break in a café or jazz club.

What village? It was named after Greenwich, southeast London, by the British colonists who settled here at the end of the 17th century. In the 18th and early 19th centuries the wealthy founders of New York society took refuge here from smallpox, cholera and yellow fever.

Bohemia, academe, jazz When the elite moved on, the bohemian invasion began, pioneered by Edgar Allan Poe, who moved to 85 W 3rd Street in 1845. Fellow literary habitués included Mark Twain, O. Henry, Walt Whitman, F. Scott Fitzgerald and Eugene O'Neill. New York University arrived in Washington Square in 1831. Post World War II, bohemia became beatnik; a group of abstract artists, centered around Jackson Pollock, Mark Rothko and Willem de Kooning, also found a home here.

Freedom parades When police raided the Stonewall Inn on June 28, 1969, and arrested gay men for illegally buying drinks, they set off the Stonewall Riots—the birth of the Gay Rights movement. The Inn was on Christopher Street, which became the main drag (no pun intended) of New York's gay community.

Union Square

For proof that New York is always evolving, see Union Square. A "needle park" in the 1970s, it's now where downtown and uptown meet, with great restaurants, a wild café scene and the city's biggest and best Greenmarket.

Not those Unions Laid out in 1839, Union Square had close encounters with socialism though its name actually refers to the union of Broadway and 4th Avenue. It was a mecca for soapbox orators in the first three decades of the 20th century, then, during the 1930 Depression, 35,000 unemployed rallied here en route to City Hall to demand work; workers' May Day celebrations convened here, too. Later, Andy Warhol picked up the vibes, set up his factory, and began publishing his style mag, *Interview*, where once the *Daily Worker* had been produced.

Green In summer, the park teems with office refugees, sharing the lawn with an equestrian George Washington by John Quincy Adams Ward, an Abe Lincoln by Henry Kirke Brown and a Marquis de Lafayette, which Frédéric-Auguste Bartholdi (of Statue of Liberty fame) gave the city in 1876. Monday, Wednesday, Friday and Saturday are Greenmarket days. An entire culture has grown around this collation of stalls overflowing with homegrown and homemade produce from New England farmers, fishers, bakers and growers. Cult highlights include maple candies, Amish cheeses, the Pretzel Man (and his pretzels), fresh clams and local honey from rooftop beehives.

THE BASICS

🔢 E15
✉ E 14th–17th streets, Park Avenue South, Broadway
🕐 Greenmarket Mon, Wed, Fri, Sat 8–6
🍴 Numerous
🚇 4, 5, 6, L, N, Q, R, W, 14th Street-Union Square
🚌 M3
♿ Poor

HIGHLIGHTS

- Saturday Greenmarket
- Union Square Café
- Jazz at Blue Water Grill
- Amish Farms stall
- Pretzel Man
- Toys R Us and Virgin Megastore
- American Savings Bank building
- Rooftop honey stall
- Apple season

More to See

BLOCK BEAUTIFUL

This picturesque, tree-lined 1920s row really is called this. Also see the pretty square nearby, centered on private Gramercy Park (see opposite page).
➕ E15 ✉ E 19th Street/Irving Place–3rd Avenue 🚇 N, R 14th Street-Union Square; 6 23rd Street

CHELSEA ART GALLERIES

The main art district is way west. ➕ B14
● **Andrea Rosen** ✉ 525 W 24th Street
☎ 212/627-6000
● **Cheim & Read** ✉ 547 W 25th Street
☎ 212/242-7727
● **Chelsea Art Museum** ✉ 556 W 22nd Street ☎ 212/255-0719
● **Gagosian** ✉ 555 W 24th Street
☎ 212/741-1111
● **Greene Naftali** ✉ 508 W 26th Street, 8th floor ☎ 212/463-7770
● **Marianne Boesky** ✉ 509 W 24th Street ☎ 212/680-9889
● **Mary Boone** ✉ 541 W 24th Street
☎ 212/752-2929
● **Matthew Marks** ✉ 522 W 22nd Street; 523 W 24th Street ☎ 212/243-0200
● **Max Protech** ✉ 511 W 22nd Street
☎ 212/633-6999
● **Paula Cooper** ✉ 534 W 21st Street
☎ 212/255-1105
● **Sean Kelly** ✉ 528 W 29th Street
☎ 212/239-1181
● **Sonnabend** ✉ 536 W 22nd Street
☎ 212/627-1018
● **Tony Shafrazi** ✉ 544 W 26th Street
☎ 212/274-9300
● **White Box** ✉ 525 W 26th Street
☎ 212/714-2347
● **White Columns** ✉ 320 W 13th Street
☎ 212/924-4212

FLATIRON BUILDING

This 1902 skyscraper was named after its amazing shape: an isosceles triangle with a sharp angle pointing uptown. This instantly recognizable and memorable landmark was designed by Daniel Burnham in 1902.
➕ E14 ✉ 175 5th Avenue/E 22nd–23rd streets 🚇 N, R 23rd Street

GRACE CHURCH

An outstanding James Renwick-designed Gothic Revival church of the first half of the 19th century.

The iconic Flatiron Building

Detail of the interior of Grace Church

The stained glass is superb, as is the mosaic floor. The original steeple, constructed in wood, was replaced by a marble one in 1888.

🔲 E16 ✉ 802 Broadway ☎ 212/254-2000 🕐 Mon–Fri 10–4, Sun services 🚇 N, R, W, 8th Street-NYU; 6 Astor Place

GRAMERCY PARK HISTORICAL DISTRICT

Peaceful and pleasant to stroll in, Gramercy is centered on the eponymous park. The park is private, locked to all but the residents of the surrounding square. The elegant National Arts Club (15 Gramercy Park South/20th Street, tel 212/475-3424) has frequent events open to non-members.

🔲 E15 🚇 N, R, 6 23rd Street

MEATPACKING DISTRICT

Bordered roughly by Jane and W 13th streets and 9th Avenue/Greenwich Street, this district was named for its wholesale meat warehouses. Then, around the millennium, the area got so hip so fast, it quickly became not hip at all. But its tangle of boutiques, bars, clubs and restaurants is still something of a magnet for young New Yorkers.

🔲 C16 🚇 A, C, E, L 14th Street

ST. MARKS-IN-THE-BOWERY

The church was built on the site of Peter Stuyvesant's chapel on his farm (*bouwerie*). His grandson sold parcels of the land in today's East Village, and the church purchased the site for the nominal fee of a dollar. Stuyvesant and many of his descendants are buried in the churchyard.

🔲 F16 ✉ E 10th Street/2nd Avenue ☎ 212/674-6377 🕐 Events only 🚇 6 Astor Place

WASHINGTON SQUARE: "THE ROW" AND THE ARCH

"The Row" (1–13 north side) housed movers and shakers of 19th-century New York City—read Henry James' *Washington Square*. At the heart of the park is the Arch, designed by Stanford White, where you can watch New Yorkers enjoying themselves.

🔲 D17 🚇 N, R 8th Street-NYU; A, C, E, B, D, F, W 4th Street-Washington Square

Entertainment in Washington Square, Greenwich Village

Metropolitan Life Insurance Building

Greenwich Village

Greenwich and West Village from then till now.

DISTANCE: 1.5 miles (2.5km) **ALLOW:** 35 minutes

START

WASHINGTON SQUARE
🚏 E17 🚇 A, B, C, D, F, V, W 4th Street

END

AVENUE OF THE AMERICAS
🚏 D15 🚇 B, D 14th Street

❶ Start in Washington Square Park and walk under the Arch, then three blocks north along 5th Avenue. Turn left into W 10th Street until you reach the Avenue of the Americas.

❽ To reach the subway go north on Washington again and turn right on W 14th to the A, C, E, L on the corner of 8th Avenue.

❷ Cross the avenue and continue on W 10th, passing the ornate Jefferson Market Library built in 1877. Ahead is 4 Patchin Place, the home of the poet e e cummings.

❼ Walk until you see the Hudson River across West Side Highway. Continue north three blocks up West Street and turn right on Bethune. At Washington turn left and in four blocks you'll be in the Meatpacking District. Explore the cobbled streets.

❸ Turn left onto Greenwich Avenue and continue until you reach the junction with Christopher Street, where you turn right and pass many cute homewares boutiques.

❻ Continue on Bleecker for four blocks. Just before W 11th Street, stop for cupcakes at the Magnolia Bakery then turn left on 11th, walk two blocks and go left on Greenwich Street, taking the next right on Perry.

❹ Stop at Christopher Park and say hello to the realistic quartet of bronze people on a bench, by George Segal, commemorating the gay rights riots nearby.

❺ Exit the park on Christopher Street, cross 7th Avenue, continue for one block, turn right on Bleecker Street.

WALK

DOWNTOWN

Shopping

ABC CARPET AND HOME

Here are seven floors of meticulously edited homewares, from four-poster beds to handkerchiefs, which share an esthetic that mixes Victorian brothel, mid-19th-century design museum, Venetian palace and deluxe hotel.

✚ E15 ✉ 888 Broadway/19th Street ☎ 212/473-3000 Ⓜ 4, 5, 6, N, Q, R, W 14th Street-Union Square

CHELSEA MARKET

More than a store, this enormous city-block-size building is several villages' worth of food boutiques, bakeries, cafés, coffee shops and delis under one roof. Even if you're not hungry, stroll through for the architect-honed industrial warehouse meets ancient cave atmosphere.

✚ C15 ✉ 75 9th Avenue/15th Street ☎ 212/243-6005 Ⓜ A, C, E, L 14th Street

CYNTHIA ROWLEY

Adorable, hip dresses and shoes. Shop here for a night out on the town.

✚ C16 ✉ 376 Bleecker Street (between Perry and Charles streets) ☎ 212/242-3803 Ⓜ 1 Christopher Street-Sheridan Square

DSW AND FILENE'S

That's "Designer Shoe Warehouse" with Prada, Kate Spade, Via Spiga et al. represented. Upstairs is a three-story Filene's

where Dolce & Gabanna, Alberta Feretti and Stella McCartney are among the labels with regular off-price off-season items.

✚ E15 ✉ 4 Union Square South (University Place) ☎ 212/674-2146 Ⓜ L, N, Q, R, W, 4, 5, 6 Union Square

GREENMARKET

Farmers travel from the tri-state area to this outdoor farmers' market that has rejuvenated the entire Union Square area.

✚ D15–E15 Ⓞ Mon, Wed, Fri, Sat 8–6 Ⓜ 4, 5, 6, N, R, L Union Square

JEFFREY NEW YORK

The coolest thing in the Meatpacking District is this compact department store of fashion so high it has vertigo. A resident DJ, a spacious all-white interior, a small but trendy cosmetics department

<table>
<tr><td>BAGEL PEOPLE</td></tr>
<tr><td>In many cities across the country you can find bagels in such unusual flavors as blueberry, chocolate or apple crumb. Not so in any self-respecting New York bagel store. Bagels are a serious matter and they are debated fiercely–there are Ess-A-Bagel people and there are H&H people. While these are the reigning kings, there are a couple of others that are worth their salt, or poppy seeds.</td></tr>
</table>

and nonpushy assistants make for a pleasant visit—and an expensive one if you fall for the wares.

✚ B15 ✉ 449 W 14th Street/Washington Street ☎ 212/206-1272 Ⓜ A, C , E, L 14th Street

LOEHMANN'S

Top designer fashions and labels at hugely reduced prices. Check out the Back Room on the 5th floor. There's another branch on the Upper West Side (Broadway at 73rd Street).

✚ D15 ✉ 101 7th Avenue/17th Street ☎ 212/352-0856 Ⓜ 1 18th Street

MARC JACOBS

Fashion's favorite darling put once-Bohemian Bleecker Street on the map.

✚ C16 ✉ 1385, 403, 405 Bleecker Street ☎ 212/924-0026 Ⓜ 1, 2 Christopher Street-Sheridan Square

PAUL SMITH

Magnificent, expensive menswear for the fashion conscious gentleman.

✚ E15 ✉ 108 5th Avenue/16th Street ☎ 212/627-9770 Ⓜ 4, 5, 6, N, R, L 14th Street-Union Square

SCOOP

Hip labels from Daryl K to Tocca and Katayone Adeli, plus cult items like James Perse T's.

✚ B15 ✉ 430 W 14th Street/Washington Street ☎ 212/691-1905 Ⓜ A, C, E 14th Street

Entertainment and Nightlife

APT

Part club, part music venue, part apartment, this hidden (no sign) swanky lounge hosts some wild nights.

⊞ C16 ⊠ 419 W 13th Street/9th Avenue ☎ 212/414-4245 🎧 A, C 14th Street

BLUE NOTE

www.bluenote.net

Top jazz artists from around the world play two shows nightly at this intimate Village jazz club and restaurant.

⊞ D17 ⊠ 131 W 3rd Street/6th Avenue–MacDougal Street ☎ 212/475-8592 🎧 A, C, E, B, D, F, W 4th Street-Washington Square

DUPLEX

Drag queens and downtown crooners sit around the piano bar and have a great time.

⊞ D17 ⊠ 61 Christopher Street/7th Avenue ☎ 212/255-5438 🎧 1 Christopher Street

GOTHAM COMEDY CLUB

Venue for up-and-coming comedians.

⊞ C14 ⊠ 208 W 23rd Street/7th Avenue ☎ 212/367-9000 🎧 N, R, I 23rd Street; F, Path 23rd Street

JOE'S PUB

The red velvet bar and performance space named after Joseph Papp, founder of the theater that houses it, has an always-interesting line-up of torch singers, comedians, magicians and new wave burlesque artistes.

⊞ E16 ⊠ The Public Theater, 425 Lafayette Street/Astor Place ☎ 212/967-7555 🎧 N, R, W 8th Street-NYU; 6 Astor Place

MERCER HOTEL LOBBY BAR

The friendly service at this tiny SoHo hot spot makes for a pleasant, chic experience.

⊞ E18 ⊠ 147 Mercer Street/Prince Street ☎ 212/966-6060 🎧 N Prince Street

MERCURY LOUNGE

A laid-back atmosphere that suits eclectic performers. Very few seats.

⊞ F17 ⊠ 217 E Houston Street/Avenue A ☎ 212/260-4700 🎧 F 2nd Avenue

O BAR

The bar of Ono, the Japanese restaurant in the Gansevoort Hotel that functions as an anchor for Meatpacking madness, is as gorgeous to look at as its patrons, but better than the gold-walled interior is the terrace garden—a mob scene on a summer Thursday night.

⊞ C16 ⊠ 18 9th Avenue/13th Street ☎ 212/660-6766 🎧 A, C, E, L 14th Street

PERFORMING GARAGE

The home of the avant-garde productions of the Wooster Group, led by Elizabeth LeCompte and often featuring her husband, Willem Dafoe.

⊞ E19 ⊠ 33 Wooster Street/Grand Street ☎ 212/966-9796 🎧 A, C, E, J, M, N, Q, R, W, Z, 1, 6 Canal Street

PETE'S TAVERN

This 1864 Gramercy Park Victorian saloon is where O. Henry wrote *The Gift of the Magi*. No matter how hokey its history, it remains a favorite, thanks to brick walls, dim light and a welcoming feel.

⊞ E15 ⊠ 129 E 18th Street/Irving Place ☎ 212/473-7676 🎧 N, R, 4, 6 14th Street-Union Square

PS 122

A converted public school that hosts a range of acts from bizarre to poignant.

⊞ F16 ⊠ 150 1st Avenue/E 9th Street ☎ 212/477-5288 🎧 N, R 8th Street, F 2nd Avenue

CABARET

The term has undergone so many image-overhauls, it's now settled into being a catch-all for entertainment options ranging from women-only male burlesque shows (Times Square Hunks, 135 W 41st Street, 212/278-0631) to drag queen lip-synching and, in the case of Lips (2 Bank Street, 212/675-7710), Bitchy Bingo. Joe's Pub (left) is among the venues that often offer what you might call classic, though modernized, cabaret.

Restaurants

PRICES

Prices are approximate, based on a 3-course meal for one person.
$$$ over $60
$$ $40–$60
$ under $40

BETTE ($$)

With carpet and art deco chandeliers on the ceiling, nightlife queen (Bungalow 8, Lot 61) Amy Sacco's restaurant feels homey—which isn't so surprising since it's named after her mom. The food is comfy, too: chicken-liver dumplings; lobster ravioli; strip steak with truffled fries and an amazing Valrhona chocolate pudding.
➕ B14 ✉ 461 W 23rd Street/9th–10th avenues ☎ 212/366-0404 🚇 A, C, E 23rd Street

DEL POSTO ($$$)

Mario Batali is New York's rotundly ebullient TV-friendly patron saint of interesting Italian food, known for rustic dishes and casual ambience. In his early-2006 latest, though, he changed the rules: This is a swanky, deco-looking, grown-up, big-night-out grand restaurant, with piano player, theatrical tableside preparations and what may be NYC's only valet parking. Of course, it works beautifully.
➕ B15 ✉ 85 10th Avenue/16th Street

☎ 212/497-8090 🚇 A, C, E, L 14th Street

GOTHAM BAR AND GRILL ($$$)

This restaurant epitomizes New York grandeur, with world-class dishes like rack of lamb with swiss chard and roasted shallots. The soaring space is light and airy with modern chandeliers.
➕ E16 ✉ 12 E 12th Street/5th Avenue ☎ 212/620-4020 🕐 Closed Sat, Sun lunch 🚇 N, R, 4, 6 Union Square

GRAMERCY TAVERN ($$–$$$)

Gramercy is laid-back, especially if you eat in the less expensive no-reservations area in front, where the food is more rustic. Tom Colicchio uses only the freshest market produce in his hearty, utterly reliable new-American food.

GIANT SUSHI

For the sushi connoisseur, Yama ($–$$) may not offer the best there is, but it does serve the biggest sushi and it is very good. Sadly, many people share this view, and the tiny place is engulfed with salivating sushi wolves, lining up for hours–you have been warned.
➕ E15 ✉ 49 Irving Place/17th Street ☎ 212/475-0969 🕐 Closed Sun 🚇 N, R, 4, 5, 6 14th Street-Union Square

➕ E15 ✉ 42 E 20th Street/Broadway–Park avenues ☎ 212/477-0777 🚇 6, N, R 23rd Street

MARY ANN'S ($)

Homemade Mexican food right down to the fresh tortillas and salsa, with dishes you won't find at your average Tex-Mex. South of the border atmosphere and margaritas by the pint at this laid-back Chelsea restaurant.
➕ C15 ✉ 116 8th Avenue/16th Street ☎ 212/633-0877 🚇 C, E 14th Street; L 8th Avenue

THE SPOTTED PIG ($$)

You're likely to wait an hour or two for a table (you can't reserve) at this Michelin-starred, Anglo-style gastro-pub. Come at off-hours, and order the gnudia kind of ricotta-spinach gnocchi that chef April Bloomfield has made her own.
➕ D16 ✉ 314 W 11th Street/Greenwich Avenue ☎ 212/620-0393 🚇 I, C, E 14th Street; 1 Christopher Street

VESELKA ($)

Ukrainian and Polish soul food 24 hours a day at this East Village institution. The extensive menu ranges from handmade pierogis to goulash, blintzes to breakfast plates. Great atmosphere.
➕ F16 ✉ 144 2nd Avenue/E 9th Street ☎ 212/228-9682 🚇 6 Astor Place

Definitely a must for visitors to Manhattan, this district has leading museums, a revitalized Times Square, Grand Central Terminal plus the magnet for shoppers— Fifth Avenue with its legendary emporiums.

Chrysler Building

HIGHLIGHTS

- Spire
- Ceiling mural
- Elevator cabs
- Fourth setback gargoyles
- African marble lobby

TIP

- From here Grand Central Terminal (▷ 58–59) is no distance at all. Head to the Food Court or Oyster Bar for lunch.

"Which is your favorite New York building?" goes the annoying yet perennial question. Nine out of ten people who express a preference pick the Chrysler Building. This should surprise nobody who gazes on it.

King for a year The tower, commissioned from William Van Alen by Walter Chrysler (who asked for something "taller than the Eiffel Tower"), won the world's tallest building competition in 1930—until the Empire State Building went up the next year. Van Alen had been almost beaten by Craig Severance's Bank of Manhattan tower at 40 Wall Street, when his rival, aware of the unofficial race, slung on an extra two feet. Unknown to Severance, though, Van Alen was constructing a 123ft (37m) stainless-steel spire, which he

The Chrysler Building viewed from the Empire State Building (left); the gleaming lobby (middle); detail of the Chrysler Building's stainless steel spire (below)

"slotted" out through the 925 ft (282 m) roof, beating the 927-footer hands down. It is ironic that the best view of the art deco beauty's top is from the observatory at the Empire State.

Multistory car Every detail of the 77-story building evokes a 1929 Chrysler Plymouth, to be exact. The winged steel gargoyles are modeled on its radiator caps; the building's stepped setbacks carry stylized hubcaps and the entire spire resembles a radiator grill; and this ain't no Toyota. The golden age of cars is further evoked by the stunning lobby, which you can visit to see the art deco detailing in the red marble, granite and chrome interior, surmounted by the 97ft by 100ft (30m by 31m) mural depicting industrial scenes and celebrating "transportation." Don't miss the marquetry elevator doors.

THE BASICS

☩ E11
✉ 405 Lexington Avenue/ 42nd Street
🕐 Mon–Fri 7am–6pm; closed holidays
🚇 4, 5, 6, 7, S Grand Central-42nd Street, Grand Central
🚌 M101, M102
🚆 Metro North, Grand Central
♿ Good
🎟 Free

Empire State Building

TOP 25

HIGHLIGHTS

- The view: by day, at dusk and by night
- The view up from 34th Street
- TowerCams
- Observatory Audio Tour
- Lights on the top stories

TIP

- The colored lights at the summit were introduced in 1976 and are changed to mark different events. You can avoid the line (though not the security one) by printing out advance tickets from the website.

It was not Fay Wray's fault, nor Cary Grant's in *An Affair to Remember*, that this is the most famous skyscraper in the world. Rather, its fame is the reason it has appeared in every New York movie. You have to climb this.

King for 40 years This is the very definition of "skyscraper," and it was the highest man-made thing until the late, lamented World Trade Center was built in the 1970s. Now it is once again the tallest building in New York. Construction began in 1929, not long before the great Wall Street Crash, and by the time it was topped out in 1931—construction went at the superfast rate of four stories a week—so few could afford to rent space, they called it "the Empty State Building." Only the popularity of its observatories kept the wolves from the

The Empire State Building (left and below); the buildings of Midtown look small when viewed from the Empire State Building (middle top); the lobby (middle left); the observation deck (middle right)

door. These viewpoints still attract 3.8 million visitors each year. The 86th floor Observatory, with its glass-enclosed, climate-controlled area, is a highlight, but if you can't make the trip, the live online ESB TowerCams provide a live video feed of the view from the very top.

Facts It is 1,250ft (381m) high, with 102 floors. The frame contains 60,000 tons of steel, 10 million bricks line the building, and there are 6,500 windows. The speediest of the 73 elevators climb 1,200ft (355m) per minute. The fastest runners in the annual Empire State Run-Up climb almost 170 steps per minute, making the 1,860 steps to the 102nd floor in 11 minutes—the steps are no longer open to the public. The highest observation deck on the 102nd floor has reopened but requires a separate ticket and an additional fee.

THE BASICS

www.esbnyc.com

✚ D13

✉ 350 5th Avenue/ W 34th Street

☎ 212/736-3100

🕐 Daily 8am–2am; last admission 1.15am

🍴 Snack bar

🚇 B, D, F, N, Q, R, V, W, 34th Street-Herald Square

🚌 M1, M2, M3, M4, M5, M16, M34

🚉 PATH 33rd Street

♿ Good

💲 Expensive

Fifth Avenue

HIGHLIGHTS

● Shopping!
● Empire State Building
● Rockefeller Center
● The Met
● The Guggenheim
● The Cooper-Hewitt

TIP

● Try to see a parade—
St. Patrick's Day Parade, the
biggest, is on March 17.

Think of shopping in New York and Fifth Avenue is likely to be your next thought. But there is more here: Museums, smart hotels, private clubs and landmark buildings rub shoulders with FAO Schwartz, Tiffany's, Cartier and Saks Fifth Avenue.

Tradition and invention Fifth Avenue runs all the way from Washington Square Park up past Central Park and it houses some of the most pricey and notable real estate in New York. Walk along the avenue and you'll pass the Flatiron Building (▷ 42), Empire State Building (▷ 54), the New York Public Library (▷ 61), the Rockefeller Center (▷ 62), the Metropolitan Museum of Art (▷ 80), the Guggenheim (▷ 78), St. Patrick's Cathedral (▷ 66) and the Cooper-Hewitt (▷ 76). These are just a few of the buildings that

Fifth Avenue on the street (left) and up in the air during a parade (below)

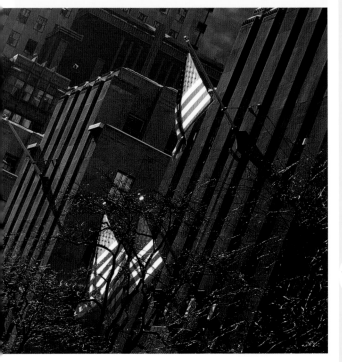

represent the development of Fifth Avenue from a sought-after address lined with mansions of the wealthy to an important artery of this vibrant city.

Shop, shop, shop The shopping venues that favor kids will be the reinvented FAO Schwarz and the Disney Store. Parents might prefer the jewelry emporia of Tiffany & Co. and Cartier, and the famous department stores. Saks Fifth Avenue has been at its Renaissance-style building (opposite Rockefeller Center) since 1922. The poshest store of all, Bergdorf Goodman, is at 57th Street, and fashion mecca Henri Bendel is at 56th.

Relax Two excellent hotels stand on 55th Street: the Peninsula New York, with great vistas from its Pentop Bar and Terrace Grill, and the St-Regis Hotel with the King Cole Bar.

THE BASICS

✚ D11–E11
✉ From Washington Square to the Harlem River
🚇 4, 5, 6
🚌 M1, M2, M3, M4

Grand Central Terminal

HIGHLIGHTS

- Main Concourse ceiling
- Oyster Bar
- The Food Court
- Mercury on the 42nd Street facade
- The clock
- The 75ft (23m) arched windows
- Grand Staircase

TIP

- Immortalize yourself at the Story Booth in the Biltmore Room next to tracks 41 and 42: it's the flagship of the remarkable oral history project (www.storycorps.net).

Don't call it a station. All tracks terminate here, which makes this—yes—a terminal. The Beaux-Arts building bustles like no place else. As the saying goes—stand here long enough and the entire world passes by.

Heart of the nation "Grand Central Station!" bellowed (erroneously) the 1937 opening of the eponymous NBC radio drama; "Beneath the glitter and swank of Park Avenue…Crossroads of a million private lives!…Heart of the nation's greatest city…" And so it is, and has been since 1871 when the first, undersize version was opened by Commodore Cornelius Vanderbilt, who had bought up all the city's railroads, just like on a giant Monopoly board. See him in bronze below Jules-Alexis Coutans' allegorical statuary on the

The busy main concourse at Grand Central Terminal (left); the entrance to the terminal (below); detail of the clock (bottom left); people riding the escalator (bottom right)

main facade (south, 42nd Street). The current building dates from 1913 and is another Beaux Arts glory, its design modeled partly on the Paris Opéra by architects Warren and Wetmore. William Wilgus was the logician responsible for traffic-marshaling, while Reed & Stem were the overall engineers. Look up at the main concourse ceiling for the stunning sight of 2,500 "stars" in a cerulean sky, with medieval-style zodiac signs by French artist Paul Helleu.

Look within The fame of the four-faced clock atop the information booth is out of proportion to its size. Below ground is a warren of 32 miles (52km) of tracks, tunnels and vaulted chambers; in one the famed Oyster Bar resides. The Food Court is virtually a new neighborhood. Be careful what you say here—the acoustics are amazing.

THE BASICS

www.grandcentralterminal.com

➕ E11

✉ Park Avenue/E 42nd Street

☎ 212/532-4900; Story Booth 800/850-4406

🕐 Daily 5.30am–1.30am; Story Booth daily 24 hours

🍴 Restaurant, café/bar, snack bars

🚇 4, 5, 6, 7, S Grand Central-42nd Street

🚌 M101, 102 Grand Central

🚆 Metro North, Grand Central

♿ Good 🖐 Free

❓ Tours Wed 12.30pm. Meet by information booth in main concourse

☎ 212 /340-2345

Museum of Modern Art

Views of MoMA (left and middle); David and Peggy Rockefeller Building (below)

THE BASICS

www.moma.org

➕ D10

✉ 11 W 53rd Street/ 5th–6th avenues

☎ 212/708-9400

🕙 Sat–Mon, Wed, Thu 10.30–5.30, Fri 10.30–8

🍴 Restaurant

Ⓔ E, V 5th Avenue/53rd Street; B, D, F, V 47th–50th streets-Rockefeller Center

🚌 M1, 2, 3, 4, 5

💲 Expensive; free Fri 4–8

HIGHLIGHTS

● *Water Lilies*, Monet (1920)
● *Dance*, Matisse (1909)
● *Les Demoiselles d'Avignon*, Picasso (1907)
● *Starry Night*, Van Gogh (1889)
● *Broadway Boogie-Woogie*, Mondrian (1942–43)
● *One*, Pollock (1950)
● *Flag*, Jasper Johns (1954–55)

Opened in November 2004, the new MoMA building, designed by Japanese architect Yoshio Taniguchi, has been called a work of art, and at 630,000sq ft (58,527sq m) it has nearly twice the capacity of the old museum.

Van Gogh to Man Ray Founded on the 1931 bequest of Lillie P. Bliss, which consisted of 235 works, the collections now amount to about 100,000 pieces. These include household objects, photography, graphic design, conceptual art and industrial design.

Postimpressionists to graffiti artists The collection starts in the late 19th century, with the Postimpressionists and Fauvists. Among the 20th-century movements represented are Cubism, Futurism, Expressionism, Surrealism, Abstract Expressionism, Pop (Oldenburg, Dine, Rauschenberg and Warhol) and the "Graffiti" work of Keith Haring and Jean-Michel Basquiat.

Even more modern A sunlighted 110ft (33m) high atrium affording a view of the beloved Abby Aldrich Rockefeller Sculpture Garden heralds the all-new MoMA, featuring much use of glass, granite, aluminum and floods of light. Taniguchi designed individual galleries specifically for the media they house, including new ones for contemporary art and new media. A restaurant operated by restaurateur Danny Meyer raises the glamour quotient, that is, if this modern art collection didn't already do so.

A nearly full Reading Room (below); sign on the outside of the building (right)

Why are we sending you to a library on your vacation? Because the New York Public Library's Central Research Building is a great, white, hushed palace, beautiful to behold even if you have no time to open a book.

The building Carrère and Hastings (who also designed the Frick, ▷ 77) were the architects of what is generally thought the city's best representative of the Beaux Arts style—the sumptuous yet classical French school that flourished from 1880 to 1920 in New York. A pair of lions, which Mayor LaGuardia christened Patience and Fortitude, flank the majestic stair that leads directly into the vaulted, carved white marble temple of Astor Hall. The lions are themselves flanked by fountains, "Truth" and "Beauty." Behind this briefly stood New York's version of London's Crystal Palace, built for the first American World's Fair in 1853. Like the London one, it burned down. Inside, see temporary exhibitions in the Gottesman Hall, and look up! The carved oak ceiling is sublime; read in the two-block-long Main Reading Room; see library collection rarities in the Salomon Room; and don't miss the Richard Haas murals of NYC publishing houses in the De Witt Wallace Periodical Room.

The books The library owns more than 15 million books, most living in the 82 branches. This building is dedicated to research. The CATNYP computer can disgorge any of the 16 million manuscripts or 3 million books from the 92 miles (148km) of stacks in 10 minutes flat.

THE BASICS

www.nypl.org

⊞ D11

✉ 476 5th Avenue/42nd Street

☎ 212/930-0830

🕐 Mon, Thu–Sat 11–6; Tue–Wed 11–7.30, Sun 1–5; closed holidays

🍴 Kiosks outside (not winter)

🚇 4, 5, 6, 7, S Grand Central-42nd Street

🚌 M1, M2, M4, M5, M42

🚆 Metro North, Grand Central

♿ Good

🎫 Free

HIGHLIGHTS

● Patience and Fortitude
● "Truth" and "Beauty"
● T. S. Eliot's typescript of *The Waste Land*
● Jefferson's handwritten Declaration of Independence
● Astor Hall
● Thomas Hastings' flagpost bases
● Gottesman Hall ceiling

Rockefeller Center

People outside the center (left); Prometheus statue (middle) beside the ice rink (below)

THE BASICS

www.rockefellercenter.com

🔆 D10

✉ 5th–7th Avenues/ 47th–52nd streets

☎ 212/632-3972

🕐 Various

🍴 Many restaurants, cafés

🚇 B, D, F, V 47th–50th streets-Rockefeller Center

🚌 M1, M2, M3, M4, M5, M27, M50

♿ Moderate

🎟 Free

www.topoftherocknyc.com

☎ 212/698-2000

🕐 Daily 8.30am–midnight (last shuttle 11pm)

🎟 Expensive

❓ Radio City tours ☎ 212/ 247-4777; NBC Studio and Rockefeller Center tours ☎ 212/664–3700

HIGHLIGHTS

● Top of the Rock Observation Deck
● GE Building's lobbies
● NBC Studio tour
● Skating in winter
● Radio City Music Hall
● *Prometheus* (1934)
● *Atlas* (5th Avenue, 50th–51st streets)

This small village of famous art deco buildings provides many of those "Gee, this is New York" moments, especially in winter when you see ice-skaters ringed by the flags of the UN and gaze up at the massive tree.

Prometheus **is here** The 19-building Rockefeller Center has been called "the greatest urban complex of the 20th century." John D. Rockefeller Jr.'s grand real estate scheme provided work for a quarter of a million souls during the Depression. Its centerpiece is the elongated ziggurat GE Building (formerly the RCA building) at 30 Rockefeller Plaza, adorned with Lee Lawrie's glass-and-limestone frieze, lobby murals by José Maria Sert and other artworks. Rest on a Channel Gardens bench and gaze on the lower plaza, the rink and Paul Manship's *Prometheus*.

Top of the Rock The three-tiered observation deck at the top of the GE building affords stunning panoramic views over Manhattan and the only such public view over Central Park. The mezzanine museum gives historical highlights of the complex before high-speed elevators whisk you to the 67th–70th floor viewing platforms at the very top.

Conan and Rockettes The GE Building also houses NBC Studios. Take a studio tour or join the queue for standby tickets to the popular talk show "Late Night with Conan O'Brien." Over on Avenue of the Americas is Radio City Music Hall, landmark home to the Rockettes.

Times Square

"The Crossroads of the World," one-time symbol of Manhattan glitz and glam, is an area New Yorkers love to hate—especially since it has been sanitized. You may disagree as you explore the big stores and get dazzled by the neon.

Longacre The junction of Broadway and 7th Avenue wasn't even called Times Square until 1904. It was "The Longacre" until Times Tower, the new home of the *New York Times*, was finished. Almost immediately, the invention of neon light, the opening of the first subway line and the decision to site the city's New Year celebration here conspired to make the triangular square the de facto center of Manhattan.

On Broadway The theaters moved in and Broadway, the Great White Way, became synonymous with bigtime showbiz: popular theatrical—especially musical—division. By 1914 there were 43 theaters in the immediate vicinity; after multiple closings, refurbishments and reopenings, there are some 22 of them today.

Best of Times, Worst of Times By the 1970s Times Square was one of the most crime-ridden neighborhoods in the city, rife with porn emporia of all kinds, drug-dealing and assorted vileness. The dawn of the 1990s saw the rebirth with several city-run and independent organizations working to clean up and reglamorize. As the giant stores, state-of-the-art illuminations and even the Armed Forces recruiting station show, it worked.

Shopping Spree

THE BASICS

SoHo Crawl
🚇 N, R, W, Prince Street

Madison Avenue
🚇 F Lexington Avenue/
63rd Street

HIGHLIGHTS

● Areas not covered here include (but are not restricted to) Herald Square (Macy's and huge branches of H&M, Old Navy, Gap, Victoria's Secret); Fifth Avenue (▷ 56); the *other* Fifth Avenue in Park Slope, plus other Brooklyn strips at Smith Street (Boerum Hill/Carroll Gardens) and Bedford Avenue (Williamsburg) all teeming with enchanting independent boutiques. Then there's Nolita, the grid of dinky high-fashion stores centered on Elizabeth Street; the multiple hipster emporia of the Lower East Side and the "big box" stores of Chelsea.

What is great about shopping in New York is the way you come across cool stores all over the place, and also the sheer quantity of shopping neighborhoods. Here is an easy two-part shopping mission that you can manage (just about) in one day.

SoHo crawl Start with a coffee and pastry at Dean and DeLuca (Broadway/Prince). You're opposite the museumlike Prada store with Kate's Paperie (▷ 32) two blocks away. Huge H&M and Zara stores are also here. Head south down Broadway for Scoop (▷ 45) and branches of the underwear queen, Victoria's Secret (at Spring) and the cosmetics sweet shop Sephora (555 Broadway); Banana Republic (women at 552, men at 528) and Old Navy; you'll also see shoe stores carrying sneakers and casual brands like Frye, Dansko and Merrill (for fabulous fashion shoes go one block east to Otto Tootsi Plohound at 273 Lafayette Street). On the east side of the street is the downtown branch of Bloomingdale's (504 Broadway). Now head down Broome, stopping at Gourmet Garage (▷ 32) for a snack, check out Kate Spade accessories opposite and head north on Mercer, Greene or Wooster. Here you're on your own, with lots of stores to explore.

Madison Avenue The next leg is easier. Take the F from Broadway-Lafayette Street to Lexington Avenue/63rd Street, walk west across Park Avenue to Madison Avenue and turn left. Head straight to Barneys (▷ 85), then work your way slowly down. Well done!

More to See

INTERNATIONAL CENTER OF PHOTOGRAPHY

In the heart of Midtown, the ICP is both a school and a museum. Temporary exhibitions are always on view, and the permanent collection has 60,000 photographs ranging from old daguerreotypes to iris prints, mainly from American and European reportage and documentation from the 1930s to the present. There are photographs by such well-known names as Henri Cartier-Bresson, Elliott Erwitt and Harold Edgerton, along with a collection of 13,000 original prints by Weegee, who photographed crime scenes and New York nightlife in the 1930s and 1940s.

➕ D11 ✉ 1133 Avenue of the Americas/ 43rd Street ☎ 212/857-0000 🕐 Tue–Thu 10–6, Fri 10–8, Sat–Sun 10–6 Ⓜ B, D, F, V 42nd Street 💲 Expensive

"LIPSTICK BUILDING"

This likeable 1986 show-off is by John Burgee with Philip Johnson.

➕ F10 ✉ 885 3rd Avenue/54th Street Ⓜ E, V Lexington Avenue

MADISON SQUARE GARDEN

Above Penn Station, this popular venue is for concerts and major sports events. It is also the home of the New York Knicks basketball team

➕ C13 ✉ 4 Penn Plaza ☎ 212/465-6741 Ⓜ A, C, E, 1, 2, 3, 34th Street-Penn Station

MORGAN LIBRARY

The Renzo Piano extension has doubled the library's gallery space and added a new Reading Room and Madison Avenue entrance. The collection was started by financier John Pierpont Morgan at the end of the 19th century. It includes the 9th-century Lindau Gospels, a rare vellum copy of the Gutenberg Bible, the medieval Dutch masterpiece *The Hours of Catherine of Cleves*, scores by Beethoven, Mozart and Puccini and manuscripts by authors Jane Austen, Charles Dickens, Henry David Thoreau and Mark Twain.

➕ E12 ✉ 225 Madison Avenue/E 36th Street ☎ 212/685-0008 🕐 Tue–Thu 10.30–5, Fri 10.30–9, Sat 10–6, Sun 11–6 Ⓜ 4, 5, 6 33rd Street 💲 Expensive

Inside the International Center of Photography

PALEY CENTER FOR MEDIA

The museum was established in 1989 on land donated by William S. Paley, a former chairman of broadcasting giant CBS. The archive of 100,000 tapes of programs, and commercials span nearly 100 years. When you arrive, make a reservation to use the computer catalog on the fourth floor to locate what interests you, then reserve it and watch it in one of the museum's consoles. Or you can take in a show or two at one of the screening rooms or theaters. Seminars and classes, as well as exhibitions, are held throughout the year.

✚ D10 ✉ 25 W 52nd Street ☎ 212/621-6800 ☻ Tue–Sun 12–6, Thu until 8, Fri theater programs ☻ E, V 5th Avenue/53rd Street ♨ Moderate

ST. PATRICK'S CATHEDRAL

James Renwick's Gothic Revival cathedral is the US's biggest for Roman Catholics, seating around 2,200. The beautiful St. Michael and St. Louis altar was designed by Tiffany & Co.

✚ E10 ✉ 5th Avenue/E 50th Street

☎ 212/753-2261 ☻ 6.30am–8.45pm
☻ 6 51st Street; E, V 5th Avenue/53rd Street

TRUMP TOWER

"Glitz" captured in pink marble and glass. The top floors are made up of apartments, while below is a six-floor atrium with shops, waterfalls and greenery.

✚ E9 ✉ 725 5th Avenue/56th Street
☎ 212/832-2000 ☻ 8am–10pm
🍴 Several ☻ E, N, R, V 5th Avenue

UNITED NATIONS HEADQUARTERS

The 544ft (166m) Secretariat building that dominates the site opened in 1950. Alongside are the General Assembly building, the Conference building (fronting the river) and the Dag Hammarskjöld Library. A guided tour covers the General Assembly Hall and Security Council Chamber.

✚ G11 ✉ United Nations Plaza
☎ 212/963-8687 ☻ Daily 9.30–4.45; closed weekends Jan–Feb 🍴 Restaurant
☻ 4, 5, 6, 7 Grand Central-42nd Street
♨ Expensive

St Patrick's Cathedral

Trump Tower

Midtown Stroll

A stroll that takes you past all the greatest hits of Midtown.

DISTANCE: 2 miles (3km) **ALLOW:** 40 minutes (and more for Central Park)

START ·········

MADISON SQUARE GARDEN
✚ C13 🚇 1, 2, 3 34th Street-Penn Station

········· **END**

ROCKEFELLER CENTER (▷ 62)
✚ D10 🚇 B, D, F, V 47–50th streets/
Rockefeller Center

① Take a look at Madison Square Garden, behind Penn Station a block west of the subway. Head back uptown, then take 34th Street east one block to Herald Square.

⑧ If you have the energy and the time, head north to Central Park for some more bucolic strolling.

② Macy's and Manhattan Mall are here. Toward the end of the next block, look up to your right. You're underneath the Empire State Building.

⑦ Go west on 53rd Street, then south on Madison Avenue to 50th Street, and veer west. Here is Saks Fifth Avenue and St. Patrick's Cathedral, on the right. Straight ahead you'll find the vast Rockefeller Center.

③ Head north up Fifth Avenue. Six blocks brings you to the Beaux Arts magnificence of the New York Public Library, with Bryant Park behind.

⑥ Circumnavigate Grand Central, hitting Park Avenue again at 46th Street, with the MetLife building at your back. A few blocks north are the precursors of the Manhattan skyline: Lever House and the Seagram Building.

④ Pass the library, then go east on 42nd Street until you reach Grand Central Terminal. Call in to admire the magnificent main concourse and pause for a coffee.

⑤ Continue east a block and a half and on the left is the Chrysler Building.

MIDTOWN

👣 **WALK**

Shopping

BERGDORF GOODMAN
For the most sophisticated shopping experience in New York, the eight-floor fashion-for-lunching-ladies department store in the former Vanderbilt mansion takes the cake. ✚ E9 ✉ 754 5th Avenue/57th Street ☎ 212/753-7300 Ⓢ N, R, W 5th Avenue/59th Street

COACH
The leather goods, starring handbags, purses and shoes aren't at all boringly preppy any more—not since design director Reed Krakoff took charge. Exciting shapes and colors change with the seasons. There are other branches. ✚ E10 ✉ 620 5th Avenue/50th Street ☎ 212/245-4148 Ⓢ E, V 5th Avenue/53rd Street

FAO SCHWARZ
The near-legendary toy store has lost its iconic giant clockwork tower but gained a whole new lease of life. There are plenty of areas for kids to experiment with giant toys you have no intention of dragging home. Don't forget to dance on the piano from *Big*. ✚ E9 ✉ 767 5th Avenue/58th Street ☎ 212/644-9400 Ⓢ N, R, W 5th Avenue/59th Street

MACY'S
The sign outside says it's the largest store in the world, and by the time you've made your way across the nine-block-long floors of this grandfather of all department stores, you'll believe them. Everything (including thousands of other shoppers) is here. ✚ D12 ✉ 151 W 34th Street-Herald Square ☎ 212/695-4400 Ⓢ B, D, F, N, R 34th Street

MANOLO BLAHNIK
Creations for the feet that are sought after by fashionistas and celebrities. ✚ D10 ✉ 31 W 54th Street ☎ 212/582-3077 Ⓢ E, V 5th Avenue/53rd Street

MICHAEL C. FINA
Every bride wants her list at this exclusive purveyor of gifts and tableware. ✚ E11 ✉ 545 5th Avenue/45th Street ☎ 212/557-2500 Ⓢ 4, 5, 6, 7 Grand Central

COLUMBUS CIRCLE
The closest thing to a mall in Manhattan, this splashy high-rise reclaimed drab Columbus Circle from the traffic when it opened in 2004. Upstairs are posh restaurants, plus the Mandarin Oriental hotel and a swanky health club. The lowest four levels contain the shopping experience. The *pièce de résistance* is the below-ground-level Whole Foods Market (see right)—a Texan-born upscale grocery chain.

NIKE TOWN NY
Feel like a professional athlete here. High-tech videos, multilevel displays and an industrial atmosphere encourage aerobic shopping. ✚ D9 ✉ 11 Pennsylvania Plaza (57th Street/5th Avenue) ☎ 212/891-6473 Ⓢ N, R 57th Street

SAKS FIFTH AVENUE
The flagship store of the now nationwide chain, with a fabulous range of designer fashions for men as well as women, and a great beauty department. ✚ E10 ✉ 611 5th Avenue/49th–50th streets ☎ 212/753-4000 Ⓢ E, F 5th Avenue

TAKASHIMAYA
An austere Japanese esthetic informs the atmosphere of this small but exquisite department store. Housewares and gifts are the main focus. ✚ E9 ✉ 693 5th Avenue/55th Street ☎ 212/350-0100 Ⓢ E, F 5th Avenue

WHOLE FOODS MARKET
The lower floor of the Time Warner Center is by far New York's largest food store. Find prepared food of every kind, hot bars of Indian, Latin and Asian dishes, cafés, baked goods, fish, cheeses, meat, fruit… ✚ C9 ✉ Concourse Level, Time Warner Center, Broadway (59th/60th Street) ☎ 212/823-9600 Ⓢ A, B, C, D, 1 59th Street-Columbus Circle

Entertainment and Nightlife

BIRDLAND
Big names, big bands, Coltrane tributes and Cubans is the range here. ➕ C11 ✉ 315 W 44th Street/8th–9th avenues ☎ 212/ 581-3080 🚇 A, C, E 42nd Street-Port Authority Bus Terminal

CARNEGIE HALL
This world-class recital hall features an eclectic program from classical artists to folk singers. ➕ D9 ✉ 881 7th Avenue/ 57th Street ☎ 212/247-7800 🚇 N, R 57th Street; E 7th Avenue

CAROLINE'S COMEDY CLUB ON BROADWAY
Established names and up-and-comers perform at this gold standard of clubs. Open every day. ➕ C10 ✉ 1626 Broadway/ 49th Street ☎ 212/757-4100 🚇 1 50th Street

ETHEL BARRYMORE THEATRE
Opened in 1928, this theater saw Fred Astaire perform in the 30s, at the start of his movie career. ➕ C11 ✉ 243 W 47th Street/ Broadway–8th Avenue ☎ 212/ 239-6200 🚇 1, C, E 50th Street; N, R, W, 49th Street

FOUR SEASONS HOTEL
I. M. Pei's design gives this a sleek, austere energy. Impressive Martini menu. ➕ E9 ✉ 57 E 57th Street/ Madison Avenue ☎ 212/ 758-5700 🚇 4, 5, 6 Lexington Avenue-59th Street

MADISON SQUARE GARDEN
The not-so-beautiful giant concrete circle is one of the city's major venues for music and sporting events. For the box office enter the Main Ticket Lobby at 7th Avenue and 32nd Street. ➕ C13 ✉ 4 Pennsylvania Plaza ☎ 212/465-6741 212/ 307-7171 (Ticketmaster) 🚇 1, 2, 3 34th Street-Penn Station

THE NEW VICTORY THEATER
If you have kids of any age (over 5) in tow, there'll be something here to thrill them—and, chances are, you also. It has one of the best youth-centric programs. ➕ C11 ✉ 209 W 42nd Street/7th–8th avenues ☎ 646/223-3020 🚇 1, 2, 3, 7, N, R, Q, W Times Square-42nd Street

NOKIA THEATRE
A medium-size venue for medium-big acts in the center of Times Square. ➕ C11/D11 ✉ 1515 Broadway/44th Street ☎ 212/930-1959 🚇 1, 2, 3, 7, N, Q, R, S, W Times Square-42nd Street

OAK ROOM
A wood-panel classic in a famous hotel that's not what it was in Round Table days, but is still worth a visit for the Sunday jazz brunch and evening cocktails accompanied by torch singers and the like. ➕ D11 ✉ Algonquin Hotel, 59 W 44th Street/6th Avenue ☎ 212/419-9331 🚇 1B, D, F, V 42nd Street

RADIO CITY MUSIC HALL
This landmark art deco theater hosts several music shows a year. You can take an hour-long tour and learn all about its life since it opened in 1932. ➕ D10 ✉ 1260 6th Avenue/ 50th Street ☎ 212/247-4777 🕐 Varied. Tours daily 11–3 🚇 B, D, F, V 40th–50th streets-Rockefeller Center

ROSELAND BALLROOM
Nowadays mostly hosting indie bands, this 3,500-seat ballroom has been open continuously since 1919. ➕ C10 ✉ 239 W 52nd Street/Broadway ☎ 212/247-0200 🚇 B, D, E 7th Avenue

Restaurants

PRICES

Prices are approximate, based on a 3-course meal for one person.
$$$ over $60
$$ $40–$60
$ under $40

LE BERNARDIN ($$$)

Frenchman Eric Ripert is acknowledged to be the fish maestro. Exquisite, inventive dishes are served by super-attentive waiters.
➕ D10 ✉ 155 W 51st Street/ 7th Avenue ☎ 212/ 489-1515 🄲 Closed Sat lunch, Sun 🄱 B, D, F, V 47th–50th streets-Rockefeller Center

CAFÉ GRAY ($$)

Gray Kunz's successor to Lespinasse is the warmest space in the chilly Time Warner Center. His elevated bistro food is sublime.
➕ C9 ✉ 10 Columbus Circle, 3rd floor/60th Street ☎ 212/823-6338 🄲 Open for dinner only 🄱 A, B, C, D, 1 59th Street-Columbus Circle

FOUR SEASONS ($$$)

Every once in a while a restaurant defines an age, and then transcends it. The Four Seasons changed the face of New York dining. Choose between the dark-wood-panel Grill Room and the romantic Pool Room.
➕ E10 ✉ 99 E 52nd Street/ Park–Lexington avenues ☎ 212/754-9494 🄲 Closed Sat lunch, Sun 🄱 6 51st Street

LEVER HOUSE ($–$$$)

The mid-century-modern ocean liner-esque design by Mark Newman is the star at this ultra-glamorous restaurant downstairs at the iconic 1952 building on Park Avenue, but it would be worth visiting for chef Dan Silverman's eclectic-contemporary menu alone.
➕ E10 ✉ 390 Park Avenue/53rd Street ☎ 212/888-2700 🄲 Closed Sat lunch, Sun 🄱 E, V Lexington Avenue/53rd Street; 6 51st Street

THE MODERN ($$$)

With Danny Meyer (New York's best-loved restaurateur) in charge and young star chef, Alasatian-born, Gabriel Kreuther behind the range, MoMA's fancy restaurant is not just for museum visits. Expect

TERMINAL FEEDING

Here are some highlights at the Food Court at Grand Central Terminal:
Café Spice for curries.
Caviarteria is as it sounds—fish eggs and champagne.
Custard Beach is all about the richest, bestest vanilla ice cream.
Junior's is a great diner with peerless cheesecake.
Knödel does wurst, boudin, merguez…
Mindy's Kosher Delicatessen does knishes and pastrami-on-rye.

fascinating takes on modern French food.
➕ D10 ✉ 9 W 53rd Street/5th–6th avenues ☎ 212/333-1220 🄲 Closed Sat lunch, Sun 🄱 E, V 5th Avenue/53rd Street

OYSTER BAR ($–$$)

Whether at the long counter or in the wood-paneled dining room, food in the 1913 vaulted Guastavino-tiled rooms in Grand Central is a thoroughly New York experience.
➕ E11 ✉ Grand Central Terminal, lower level ☎ 212/490-6650 🄱 4, 5, 6, 7 Grand Central-42nd Street

PER SE ($$$)

If you want to know what all the fuss is about, reserve *way* ahead for French Laundry-maestro Thomas Keller's astonishing, precise and idiosyncratic food. A table by the window with those amazing views would be the top score.
➕ C9 ✉ Time Warner Center, 10 Columbus Circle, 4th floor/60th Street ☎ 212/823-9335 🄲 Closed Mon–Thu lunch 🄱 A, B, C, D, 1 59th Street-Columbus Circle

'21' CLUB ($$$)

This restaurant has been famous from its speakeasy days.
➕ D10 ✉ 21 W 52nd Street/ 5th–6th avenues ☎ 212/ 582-7200 🄲 Closed Sun 🄱 B, D, F, V 47th–50th streets-Rockefeller Center

G E N H E I M

Central Park is the city's lungs—a huge green space for all Manhattan. Visit the zoo; see free summer Shakespeare or bring a picnic. The museums of the Upper East Side are renowned worldwide.

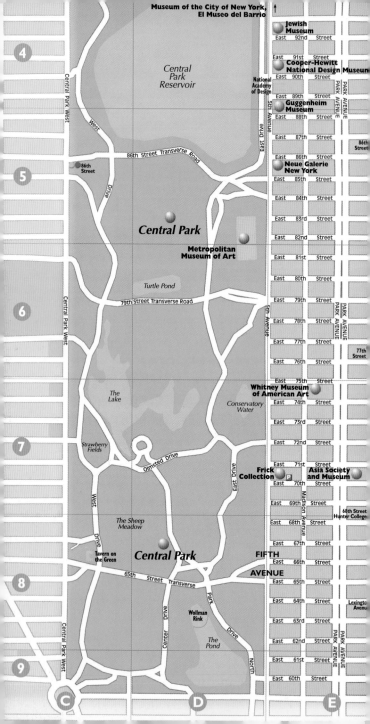

**Museum of the City of New York,
El Museo del Barrio**

**Jewish
Museum**
East 92nd Street

East 91st Street
**Cooper-Hewitt
National Design Museum**
East 90th Street

National
Academy
of Design
East 89th Street
**Guggenheim
Museum**
East 88th Street

East 87th Street

East 86th Street
**Neue Galerie
New York**
East 85th Street

86th
Street

East 84th Street

East 83rd Street

East 82nd Street

East 81st Street

**Metropolitan
Museum of Art**

East 80th Street

East 79th Street

East 78th Street

East 77th Street

77th
Street

East 76th Street

East 75th Street
**Whitney Museum
of American Art**

East 74th Street

East 73rd Street

East 72nd Street

East 71st Street
**Frick
Collection**   **Asia Society
and Museum**

East 70th Street

East 69th Street

64th Street
Hunter College

East 68th Street

East 67th Street

East 66th Street
FIFTH

East 65th Street
AVENUE

East 64th Street

Lexington
Avenue

East 63rd Street

East 62nd Street

East 61st Street

East 60th Street

*Central
Park
Reservoir*

86th Street Transverse Road

86th
Street

Central Park

Turtle Pond

79th Street Transverse Road

*The
Lake*

*Conservatory
Water*

*Strawberry
Fields*

Olmsted Drive

*The Sheep
Meadow*

Central Park

Tavern on
the Green

65th Street Transverse

Wollman
Rink

*The
Pond*

Central Park West

West   Drive

Center   Drive

Park   Drive

North   Drive

East Drive

5th Avenue

East Drive

5th Avenue

Madison Avenue

PARK AVENUE   PARK AVENUE

PARK AVENUE   PARK AVENUE

PARK AVENUE   PARK AVENUE

4

5

6

7

8

9

C

D

E

East 93rd Street
UPPER EAST
East 92nd Street
SIDE
East 91st Street
East 91st Street
East 90th Street
East 89th Street
Gracie Mansion
East 88th Street
East 87th Street
Carl Schurz Park
East 86th Street
East 85th Street
East 84th Street
East 83rd Street
East 82nd Street
East 81st Street
East 80th Street
East 79th Street
3rd Avenue
2nd Avenue
1st Avenue
York Avenue
East 78th Street
John Jay Park
East 77th Street
East 76th Street
East 75th Street
East 74th Street
East 73rd Street
East 72nd Street
East 71st Street
East 70th Street
FRANKLIN DELANO ROOSEVELT DRIVE
East
East 69th Street
East 68th Street
East 67th Street
East 66th Street
East 65th Street
East 64th Street
East 63rd Street
York Avenue
East 62nd Street
3rd Avenue
2nd Avenue
1st Avenue
East 61st St
Mount Vernon Hotel Museum and Garden
Lexington Avenue
East 60th Street
HIGHWAY 25   QUEENSBORO BRIDGE

0   300 m
0   250 yds

F

G

Central Park

HIGHLIGHTS

● Delacorte Theater,
Shakespeare in the Park
● Summer stage concerts
● Bleachers at Heckscher
● Bethesda Fountain
● Wollman Rink in winter
● Strawberry Fields
● Swedish Cottage
Marionette Theater
● Tavern on the Green

TIPS

● Don't walk alone in
isolated areas at night.
● Watch out for bicycles on
the roads.

**The park is the escape valve for the city.
Without it New York would overheat—
especially in summer, when the humidity
tops 90 percent, and bikers, runners,
bladers, dog strollers and Frisbee players
convene. It's a way of life.**

The Greensward Plan In the mid-19th century,
when there was no Manhattan north of 42nd
Street, *New York Evening Post* editor William
Cullen Bryant campaigned until the city invested
$5 million in an 840 acre (340ha) wasteland.
Responsible for clearing the land was journalist
Frederick Law Olmsted, who, with English architect
Calvert Vaux, also won the competition to design
the park, with his "Greensward Plan." By day,
Olmsted supervised the clearance of 5 million
cubic tons of dirt; by night, he and Vaux trod the

A variety of ways to enjoy the park; a view across the lake to some landmark West Side apartments, including the Dakota Building with its pointed gables (top right); the memorial to John Lennon in Strawberry Fields (bottom right)

acres and designed. Nighttime walks, though no longer suicidal, are still not advised these days.

Fun and games Start at the Dairy Information Center and pick up a map and events list. These show the layout of the park and tell you about the Wildlife Conservation Center (Zoo), the Carousel, the playgrounds, rinks, fountains, statues and Strawberry Fields, where John Lennon is commemorated close to the Dakota Building where he lived and was shot. But the busy life of the park is not recorded on maps: rollerblade moves on the Mall by the Sheep Meadow; hanging out at the Heckscher Playground and Great Lawn softball leagues; doing the loop road by bike; sunbathing, poolside, at the vast Lasker Pool in Harlem; playing rowboat dodgems on the Lake; or bouldering on the outcrops of Manhattan schist (rock).

THE BASICS

www.centralparknyc.org

+ D5

☎ 212/794-6564 or 800/201-7275

⊘ Dairy Information Center Tue–Sun 10–5

🍴 Restaurants, kiosks

Ⓐ A, B, C, D, 1 59th Street-Columbus Circle; N, Q, R, W, 57th Street-7th Avenue; F 57th Street; 4, 5, 6 86th Street

🚌 M1, M2, M3, M4, M5, M10. Crosstown M66, M30, M72, M86

♿ Moderate

💲 Free

Cooper-Hewitt National Design Museum

THE BASICS

http://cooperhewitt.org

✚ E4

✉ 2 E 91st Street

☎ 212/849-8400

🕐 Mon–Thu 10–5, Fri 10–9, Sat 10–6, Sun 12–6; closed holidays

🍴 None

Ⓠ 4, 5, 6 86th Street

🚍 M1, M2, M3, M4

♿ Good

💲 Expensive

❓ Tours available

HIGHLIGHTS

● Paneling in the hall
● Solarium
● Garden
● Architectural drawings
● Summer concerts
● Textiles
● Exhibitions

TIP

● The Shop at Cooper-Hewitt is worth visiting in its own right. Many items from the changing stock are not available elsewhere and the book section is excellent.

The charming Cooper-Hewitt National Design Museum collections are exhibited in an elegant, wood-paneled mansion. When snow falls in the holiday season, there's nowhere better to indulge in mawkishly nostalgic reveries.

Carnegie-Hewitt The mansion belonged to industrialist Andrew Carnegie, who, in 1903, had asked architects Babb, Cook & Willard for "the most modest, plainest and most roomy house in New York City." This he did not receive (aside from the roominess), since this little chateau was built with modern conveniences galore—air-conditioning and elevators—and a big gated garden to keep out the squatter neighbors. The entire neighborhood came to be known as Carnegie Hill. Andrew's wife, Louise, lived here until her death in 1946, then, some 20 years later, the Carnegie Corporation donated it to the Smithsonian Institution to house the Hewitt sisters' collections. The sisters, Amy, Eleanor and Sarah, had become infatuated with London's museums, and this set them collecting.

And Cooper The girls' grandpa Peter Cooper (▷ 38), founder of the Cooper Union college, housed the collection here, where it stayed until 1967. The contemporary Cooper-Hewitt is a vibrant institution where all kinds of events happen. Some of the collections are on display (it's hard to predict which) and there are reference resources, including the US's biggest architectural drawings collection and a textile library.

The Fifth Avenue garden (below) and Fragonard Room (right)

Frick Collection

Like the Wallace Collection in London and the Musée Picasso in Paris, Henry Clay Frick's mansion is half the reason for coming here. Henry bequeathed these riches to the nation as a memorial to himself—that's the kind of guy he was.

The mansion, and the man Henry Clay Frick was chairman of the Carnegie Steel Corp. (US Steel). He was one of the most ruthless strike-breakers of all time and the nastiest industrialist of his day. Instead of any comeuppance (though there were assassination attempts), he got to commission Carrère and Hastings to build him one of the last great Beaux Arts mansions on 5th Avenue and fill it with an exquisite collection of 14th- to 19th-century old masters, porcelain, furniture and bronzes. You can rest in a Louis XVI chair before strolling in the central glass-roofed courtyard and the gorgeous garden.

What Frick bought Some of the 40 rooms are arranged around a particular work or artist, notably the Boucher Room, east of the entrance, and the Fragonard Room, with the *Progress of Love* series. There are British masters (Constable, Gainsborough, Whistler, Turner), Dutch (Vermeer, Rembrandt, Van Eyck, Hals), Italian (Titian, Bellini, Veronese) and Spanish (El Greco, Goya, Velázquez). Interspersed are Limoges enamel and Chinese porcelain, Persian carpets and Marie Antoinette's furniture. Some Frick descendants still have keys to this modest pied à terre, which has a bowling alley in the basement.

THE BASICS

www.frick.org

➕ E7

✉ 1 E 70th Street

☎ 212/288–0700

🕐 Tue–Sun 10–6; closed holidays

🚇 6 68th Street-Hunter College

🚌 M1, M2, M3, M4

♿ Good

💲 Expensive

❓ Lectures: Wed 6pm

HIGHLIGHTS

● *Mall in St. James's Park*, Gainsborough (1783)
● *Sir Thomas More*, Holbein (1527)
● *Officer and the Laughing Girl*, Vermeer (1655–60)
● *The Polish Rider*, Rembrandt (c1655)
● *Virgin and Child with Saints*, Van Eyck (c1441–43)
● *Philip IV of Spain*, Velázquez (1644)

UPPER EAST SIDE & CENTRAL PARK

★ TOP 25

Guggenheim Museum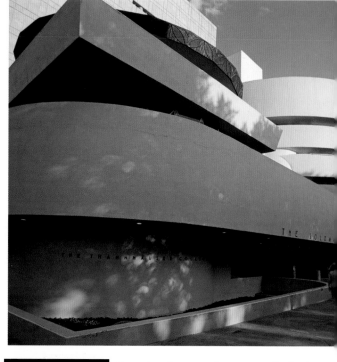

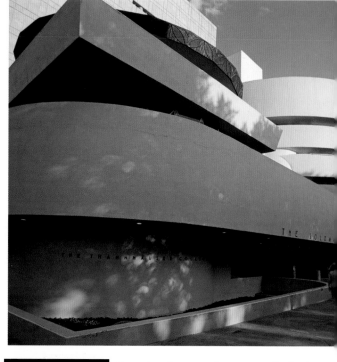

HIGHLIGHTS

- The building
- *L'Hermitage à Pontoise*, Pissarro (1867)
- *Paris Through the Window*, Chagall (1913)
- *Woman Ironing*, Picasso (1904)
- *Nude*, Modigliani (1917)
- Kandinskys
- Klees
- Légers
- The store

If you just happened across Frank Lloyd Wright's space-age rotunda, your eyes would pop out of their sockets, but it's the planet's best-known modern building, so you are prepared. Don't forget the art inside.

Museum of architecture This is the great Frank Lloyd Wright's only New York building. It was commissioned by Solomon R. Guggenheim at the urging of his friend and taste tutor, Baroness Hilla Rebay von Ehrenwiesen, though the wealthy metal-mining magnate died 10 years before it was completed in 1959. The giant white nautilus is certainly arresting, but it's the interior that unleashes the most superlatives. Take the elevator to the top level and snake your way down the museum's spiral ramp to see why. You can study the exhibits,

Exterior and interior views of the stunning design by Frank Lloyd Wright

look over the parapet to the lobby below and finish up where you began.

Museum of art There are around 6,000 pieces in the Guggenheim Foundation's possession. Solomon R. and his wife Irene Rothschild abandoned the old masters they sought at first, when Hilla Rebay introduced them to Léger, Kandinsky, Mondrian and Moholy-Nagy, Chagall and Gleizes, and they got hooked on the moderns. See also the early Picassos in the small rotunda and the 1992 tower extension. If you like the Impressionists and Postimpressionists, look for the Thannhauser Collection, always on display—unlike the rotated Guggenheim holdings. Plans for the new Guggenheim museum, designed by Frank Gehry on Piers 9, 11, 13 and 14 on the East River in Lower Manhattan, are on hold.

THE BASICS

www.guggenheim.org

🚩 E4

✉ 1071 5th Avenue/ 89th Street

☎ 212/423-3500

🕐 Sat–Wed 10–5.45, Fri 10–7.45; closed Dec 25

🍴 Café

Ⓜ 4, 5, 6 86th Street

🚌 M1, M2, M3, M4

♿ Good

💲 Expensive

❓ Lecture program

TIP

● Consider a City Pass ($65; kids $49). As well as the Gugg, it allows entry to other leading attractions. Visit www.citypass.com for information.

Metropolitan Museum of Art

HIGHLIGHTS

● Temple of Dendur (15BC)
● Period rooms, American Wing
● 19th- and early 20th-century art galleries
● *Young Woman with a Water Jug*, Vermeer (1660–67)
● *Grand Canal, Venice*, Turner (c1835)

TIP

● Consider visiting on Friday or Saturday evening, when a string quartet serenades you and there are far fewer crowds.

It will give you bigger blisters than the Uffizi, bigger chills than the Sistine Chapel and take a bigger slice of vacation time than all dinners. It's so big that it doesn't just contain Egyptian artifacts but an entire Egyptian building.

Art city The limestone Beaux Arts facade with its tremendous steps was a 1902 addition to the Calvert Vaux (of Central Park fame) redbrick Gothic building buried inside. There are several more buildings-within-buildings, interior gardens and courtyards, such is the scale of the Met. The 15BC Temple of Dendur, in its glass-walled bemoated chamber east of the main entrance, is the best known, but there's much more besides: the Astor Court above it—a replica Ming dynasty scholar's courtyard—plus, in the American Wing, a

The outside steps on a busy summer day (left); inside the main entrance of the museum with the information desk at the center (below)

score of period-style rooms, and the vast and sunlighted garden court with its hodgepodge of Tiffany glass and topiary, a Frank Lloyd Wright window and the entire Federal-style facade of the United States Bank from Wall Street.

Where to start? How to stop? A quarter of the 3 million-plus objects are up at any one time, so pace yourself. Relax. There are about 23 distinct collections. Some visitors decide on one or two per visit—Egyptian art, for example, or the new galleries for 19th- and early-20th-century European paintings which contain one of the largest Impressionist collections outside Paris. Or you could structure a route around one or two favorite works. On the gound level, the Information Center in the Uris Center, with its Orientation Theater and giant floor plans, is the place to begin.

THE BASICS

www.metmuseum.org
➕ D5
✉ 1000 5th Avenue/82nd Street
☎ 212/535-7710
🕐 Tue–Thu, Sun 9.30–5.15, Fri, Sat 9.30–8.45
🍴 Cafeteria, restaurant, bar
🚇 4, 5, 6 86th Street
🚌 M1, M2, M3, M4
♿ Good
💷 Expensive
❓ The Cloisters (▷ 106) houses more of the Met's medieval collections; same-day admission on Met ticket

Whitney Museum of American Art

HIGHLIGHTS

● Biennial
● *Circus*, Alexander Calder (1926–31)
● The Hoppers
● The O'Keeffes
● *Dempsey and Firpo*, George Bellows (1924)
● The Louise Nevelsons
● Drawbridge

TIP

● Come Friday from 6pm to 9pm. Admission is pay-what-you-wish and there are live musical performances.

More modern than the Modern, the Whitney wants to be as unpredictable as the *artist du jour* and very often succeeds. It's a New York tradition to sneer at the Biennial, whether or not you have seen the show.

No room at the Met Sculptor and patron of her contemporaries' work, Gertrude Vanderbilt Whitney offered her collection to the Met in 1929, but the great institution turned up its nose and Whitney was forced to found the Whitney. In 1966, Marcel Breuer's cantilevered, granite-clad Brutalist block was completed to house it in a suitably controversial manner—a building that is not universally loved but impossible to overlook. The Whitney's core collection now reads like a roll call of American 20th-century greats: Edward Hopper, Thomas Hart

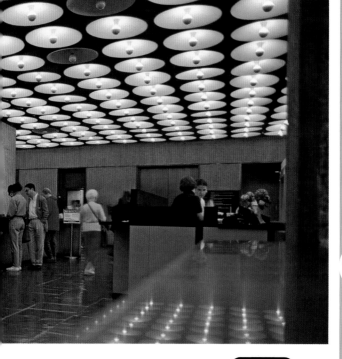

Visitors at the information and entry desks of the Whitney Museum of American Art

Benton, Willem de Kooning, Georgia O'Keeffe, Claes Oldenburg, Jasper Johns, George Bellows and Jackson Pollock are a few. Let's hope the curators and buyers are as good as Gertrude at spotting talent.

Take your pick Exhibitions, drawn from the museum's important and delicious collection, often emphasize a single artist's work. At other times they prove more eclectic. There's an active film and video department, and although the branch at the Altria Building closed in 2008, there are plans for a new building in the Meatpacking District. The Whitney Biennial (in the spring of even-numbered years) offers an echo of those days, when the New York art pack gets sweaty debating the merits and demerits of the chosen few on show and of the curator's vision.

THE BASICS

www.whitney.org

✚ E7

✉ 945 Madison Avenue/75th Street

☎ 212/570-3676

🕐 Wed–Thu, Sat–Sun 11–6, Fri 1–9; closed Thanksgiving, Dec 25, Jan 1

🍴 Café

🚇 6 77th Street

🚌 M1, M2, M3, M4

♿ Good

💲 Expensive

❓ Exhibitions, events

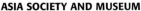

More to See

ASIA SOCIETY AND MUSEUM
This collection of Asian art and culture is based on that started by John D. Rockefeller III. The society was founded in 1956 and moved to its present headquarters in the 1980s.
⊞ E7 ⊠ 725 Park Avenue/70th Street ☎ 212/288-6400 🕐 Tue–Sun 11–6, Fri 11–9 🚇 6 68th Street 💵 Moderate

GRACIE MANSION
Gracie Mansion has been the mayor's official residence since 1942 though Mayor Bloomberg declined it. Built in 1799, it was then a remote country house. Reservations required for tours.
⊞ G4–G5 ⊠ East End Avenue/88th Street 🕐 311 or 212/639-9675 🚇 4, 5, 6 86th Street 💵 Moderate

JEWISH MUSEUM
The largest Jewish museum in the Western hemisphere chronicling Jewish experience worldwide.
⊞ E4 ⊠ 1109 5th Avenue/92nd Street ☎ 212/423-3200 🕐 Sat–Wed 11–5.45, Thu 11–8; closed Fri 🍴 Café 🚇 4, 5, 6 86th Street 💵 Expensive

EL MUSEO DEL BARRIO
New York's only museum dedicated to Latin American and Caribbean art and culture. The collection has 8,000 items and stages regular exhibitions.
⊞ E2 ⊠ 1230 5th Avenue/104th Street ☎ 212/831-7272 🕐 Wed–Sun 11–5 🚇 6 103rd Street 💵 Donation (moderate)

MUSEUM OF THE CITY OF NEW YORK
Rotating exhibitions that illustrate the changing life of the city dating back to 1624. Special walking tours are available.
⊞ E2 ⊠ 1220 5th Avenue/103rd Street ☎ 212/534-1672 🕐 Tue–Sun 10–5 🚇 6 103rd Street 💵 Donation (moderate)

NEUE GALERIE NEW YORK
Dedicated to early-20th-century German and Austrian art and design, this gallery has marvelous collections of paintings and other media.
⊞ E5 ⊠ 1048 5th Avenue/86th Street ☎ 212/628-6200 🕐 Fri 11–9, Sat–Mon, Thu 11–6 🚇 4, 5, 6 86th Street 💵 Expensive

Museum of the City of New York

Gracie Mansion bathed in winter sunshine

Shopping

BARNEYS
Many are the New Yorkers who dress exclusively from the *ne plus ultra* of high-fashion stores. Over several floors find avant-garde designers, own label clothes, the city's best high-end cosmetics and scent departments, every hip jeans label, menswear, epic shoe departments, directional jewelry, homewares, kids' clothes and more. Prices are high.
E9 ✉ 660 Madison Avenue/61st Street ☎ 212/826-8900 🚇 N, R, W 5th Avenue/59th Street

BLOOMINGDALE'S
Bloomingdale's, opened in 1879, is one of the most venerable names in Manhattan yet keeps up with every trend. The jewelry and handbag sections are excellent.
✚ F9 ✉ 1000 3rd Avenue/59th Street ☎ 212/705-2000 🚇 4, 5, 6 59th Street

CALVIN KLEIN
The iconic New York designer's flagship store, designed by David Chipperfield, is as spare and minimal as his clothing without even racks to spoil the clean lines (you point at a display and request your size). His home line is downstairs.
✚ E9 ✉ 654 Madison Avenue/60th Street ☎ 212/292-9000 🚇 N, R, W 5th Avenue/59th Street

CRATE & BARREL
Having refreshed your wardrobe, come here for the wardrobe itself, perhaps in cherrywood? Fashionable housewares and furniture at reasonable prices have made this a NY favorite.
✚ E9 ✉ Madison Avenue/59th Street ☎ 212/308-0011 🚇 N, R, W, 5th Avenue/59th Street

DONNA KARAN
This beautiful bilevel space carries the home line, accessories and the best of new season Karan, as well as her lower-price lines.
✚ E8 ✉ 819 Madison Avenue/E 68th Street ☎ 212/861-1001 🚇 6 68th Street-Hunter College

KITCHEN ARTS AND LETTERS
This is a treasure trove of cookbooks by leading authors including James Beard and Julia Child.
✚ E4 ✉ 1435 Lexington Avenue between 93rd and 94th streets ☎ 212/876-5550 🚇 6 96th Street

RALPH LAUREN
Distinguished cowboy and English country heritage looks in the Rhinelander Mansion, one of a few of such turn-of-the-20th-century houses in Manhattan.
✚ E7 ✉ 867 Madison Avenue between E 71st and 72nd streets ☎ 212/606-2100 🚇 6 68th Street-Hunter College

SHANGHAI TANG
Youthful Asian-style clothing.
✚ E8 ✉ 714 Madison Avenue between E 63rd and 64th streets ☎ 212/888-0111 🚇 F Lexington Avenue-63rd Street

ZITOMER
At root, an über-drug-store, this Upper East Side classic has grown to encompass everything from toys to pet accessories. The number and scope of bath, body and skincare ranges is impressive and it's hands-down the best place to shop for hair ornaments (OK, maybe a tie with Ricky's).
✚ E6 ✉ 969 Madison Avenue/76th Street ☎ 212/737-5560 🚇 6 77th Street

Entertainment and Nightlife

92ND STREET Y

A wonderfully varied program of events here includes readings by renowned authors, folk, jazz and lectures that cover a wide range of subjects. Celebrated its 125th anniversary in 1999.

🟦 E4 ✉ Kauffman Concert Hall, 1395 Lexington Avenue/92nd Street ☎ 212/415-5500 🟢 6 96th Street

CAFÉ CARLYLE

This lounge in the elegant Carlyle Hotel was home to the great Bobby Short, until his death in 2005, but his spirit lives on in the piano player lounge singers and jazz bands. Be sure to look in at Bemelman's Bar.

🟦 E6 ✉ Carlyle Hotel, Madison Avenue/76th Street ☎ 212/570-7189 🟢 6 77th Street

CAFÉ PIERRE

Jazz and cabaret songs, plus requests, from Nancy Winston and Kathleen Landis.

🟦 E9 ✉ 5th Avenue/61st Street ☎ 212/838-8000 🟢 N, R, W 5th Avenue/59th Street

DANGERFIELD'S

This club, established in 1969, is going strong. Those who have performed here include Jay Leno, Jim Carrey and Tim Allen.

🟦 F9 ✉ 1118 1st Avenue/61st Street ☎ 212/593-1650 🟢 4, 5, 6 59th Street

FEINSTEINS AT THE REGENCY

The cabaret star Michael Feinstein himself performs at his namesake venue only a couple of times a year but the rest of the time he manages to secure top Broadway names for this swanky, intimate room.

🟦 E9 ✉ Regency Hotel, 540 Park Avenue/61st Street ☎ 212/339-4095 🟢 N, R, W Lexington Avenue/59th Street

FLORENCE GOULD HALL

The 400-seat venue is associated with the Alliance Française. The range of events encompasses opera, jazz and pop singers, dance and readings.

🟦 E9 ✉ 55 E 60th Street/Park–Madison avenues ☎ 212/355-6100 🟢 N, R, W 5th Avenue/59th Street

---

OUT IN CENTRAL PARK

Central Park is a welcoming park. For those who crave physical activity there's lots to do.
Bike Riding You can rent a no-frills bicycle.
Roller Blading Skate rental and lessons are available at Wollman Rink.
Ice Skating Wollman Rink rents figure skates and hockey skates and is an ice rink in winter.
Running The park is the most popular place for running and jogging.

GRACE RAINEY ROGERS AUDITORIUM

A 700-seat auditorium in the Met for musical groups. Chamber music is also played in the great hall balcony of the Met on Friday and Saturday evenings.

🟦 D5 ✉ Metropolitan Museum of Art, 5th Avenue/82nd Street ☎ 212/535-7710 or 212/570-3949 🟢 4, 5, 6 86th Street

THE IRIS AND B. GERALD CANTOR ROOF GARDEN

You can get cocktails and simple food on this rooftop terrace with bits of its sponsors' sculpture collection among the wisteria trellises and a heavenly view of Central Park treetops. It's one of the nicest places for an early drink in New York. Access is via the elevators on the far southwest corner. It's open May 2 to late fall, until 4.30pm; 8.30pm Friday and Saturday.

🟦 D5 ✉ Metropolitan Museum of Art, 1000 5th Avenue/82nd Street ☎ 212/535-7710 🟢 6 86th Street

THEATER TENTEN

A rare Upper East Side off-Broadway theater. Productions range from Gilbert and Sullivan to poetry readings.

🟦 E5 ✉ 1010 Park Avenue/85th Street ☎ 212/288-3246 🟢 4, 5, 6 86th Street

Restarants

PRICES

Prices are approximate, based on a 3-course meal for one person.

$$$	over $60
$$	$40–$60
$	under $40

BOAT HOUSE ($$)

Leave Manhattan entirely at this unique lakeside place in the depths of Central Park. The food is contemporary American and it's fine but the view is the point. The cocktail deck gets predictably busy in summer. Booking advised for dinner.

➕ D7 ✉ Central Park, nearest to E 72nd Street entrance ☎ 212/517-2233 🕐 Closed major holidays and dinner Dec–Mar 🚇 6 68th Street-Hunter College

CAFÉ BOULUD ($$–$$$)

Many diners consider this to be their favorite Daniel Boulud restaurant. Three muses inspire the menu—classics, seasons and ethnic cuisines. You will find pot au feu, bouillabaisse and entrées inspired by Tuscany, Morocco, Vietnam and Spain.

➕ E6 ✉ 20 E 76th Street/5th–Madison avenues ☎ 212/772-2600 🕐 Closed Mon lunch and major holidays 🚇 6 77th Street

CAFÉ SABARSKY ($–$$)

Much more than a museum café, this—fittingly for somewhere in the patrician town house that is the Neue Galerie—looks like a 1920s Viennese Kaffeehaus and has New York's premier Austrian chef, Kurt Gutenbrunner at the helm. You can also just drop in for the *Kaffee und Kuchen*.

➕ E5 ✉ Neue Galerie New York, 1048 5th Avenue/86th Street ☎ 212/288-0665 🕐 Closed major holidays 🚇 4, 5, 6 86th Street

DANIEL ($$$)

Perhaps the most formal restaurant in the city, with its salmon-pink walls and columned arches. Serves exquisitely restrained, modern French dishes—opt for the degustation menu to fully appreciate chef Daniel Boulud's brilliance. Dessert arrives with its own "basket" of warm madeleines.

TAVERN ON THE GREEN

The Tavern delivers a memorable dining experience despite its stature as a tourist destination (colored glass, lanterns, topiary…), and despite the breadth of its menu, which ranges from prime rib with Yorkshire pudding to sautéed rainbow trout. In summer you can dance under the stars in the garden from 9pm.

➕ C8 ✉ Central Park West/67th Street ☎ 212/873-3200 🚇 1 66th Street-Lincoln Center

➕ E8 ✉ 60 E 65th Street/Madison–Park avenues ☎ 212/288-0033 🕐 Closed Sun 🚇 6 68th Street-Hunter College

JACKSON HOLE ($)

This small chain of burger places is so useful when all you want is a hefty sandwich in a child-friendly, no-frills environment after a long day hitting the museums.

➕ E4 ✉ 1270 Madison Avenue/91st Street ☎ 212/427-2820 🚇 4, 5, 6 86th Street

➕ F8 ✉ 232 E 64th Street/2nd Avenue ☎ 212/371-7187 🕐 Closed major holidays 🚇 6 68th Street-Hunter College

SERENDIPITY 3 ($)

So what if it's a cliché? This toy box/candy store of an Upper East Side institution makes the original and best "Frozen Hot Chocolate." You don't even need a child in tow but you do need a sweet tooth—and the rest of the menu is forgettable.

➕ F9 ✉ 225 E 60th Street/2nd Avenue ☎ 212/838-3531 🚇 4, 5, 6 59th Street

SUSHI OF GARI ($$$)

This highly acclaimed high-end sushi place is always full, despite high prices. Say *Omakase* to chef Gari and sharpen your tastebuds.

➕ F6 ✉ 402 E 78th Street/1st Avenue ☎ 212/517-5340 🚇 6 77th Street

West of Central Park is a largely residential, pleasantly leafy neighborhood of grand apartment buildings and big brownstones. Its major attraction is Lincoln Center, with world-class performances.

Central
Park
Reservoir

86th Street Transverse Road

West
Drive

East Drive

**Metropolitan
Museum of Art**

Central Park

Turtle Pond

79th Street Transverse Road

5th Avenue

*The
Lake*

*Conservatory
Water*

Olmsted Drive

East Drive

*The Sheep
Meadow*

Central Park

65th Street Transverse

Center Drive

Park Drive

**Wollman
Rink**

*The
Pond*

North

| 0 | | 300 m |
| 0 | | 250 yds |

D

E

American Museum of Natural History

HIGHLIGHTS

- Blue whale
- Barosaurus
- Herd of stuffed elephants
- New dinosaur halls
- Sky Shows
- Star of India
- The dioramas
- Dinosaur embryo
- "Starry Nights" jazz at the Rose Center

TIP

- You can observe the entire life cycle of tropical butterflies from October to June at the Butterfly Conservatory.

No longer a lovable anachronism since its renovation, this 19th-century hulk is stuffed with dinosaur skeletons and appended by the amazing Rose Center. The blue whale's cocktail bar and the dioramas are delightful.

Who's who Of the 36 million items owned by the museum—the largest such institution in the world—only a small fraction is on show. Among the improvements funded by a $45-million cash injection were a sprucing-up of the buildings themselves and, most notably, the metamorphosed Hayden Planetarium, now the Rose Center, next door, with its thrill ride through the universe. Another highlight is the partially interactive dinosaurs to please computer-jaded children. There's far too much to see in one day, with three

The dinosaurs are always popular, especially with children (left); the entrance of the museum (below)

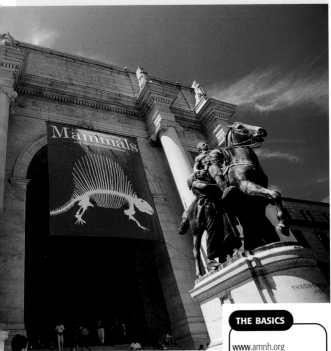

THE BASICS

www.amnh.org

🚻 C6

✉ Central Park West/
79th Street

☎ 212/769-5100

🕐 Daily 10–5.45

🍴 Various

🚇 B, C 81st Street-
Museum of Natural History

🚌 M7, M10, M11, M79

♿ Good

💲 Expensive

❓ 1-hour tours until 3.15.
Rose Center jazz and tapas
first Friday of month,
6–8.30pm

☎ 212/769-5200 for
advance reservations for
special exhibits, films, etc.

city blocks and the entire evolution of life on earth covered. Not-to-be-missed items include the barosaurus rearing up to her full 55ft (17m) to protect her young from a T-Rex attack and the 94ft (29m) blue whale that dominates the two-story Hall of Ocean Life and Biology of Fishes.

More gems Another highlight is the 563-carat Star of India sapphire, part of the unbelievable Hall of Meteorites, Minerals and Gems, containing almost $50-million worth of precious stones, plus the 34-ton Ahnighito meteorite. The cutest part of the museum is where animals of all sizes are displayed behind glass in *tableaux morts* of great artistic merit. In the Nature Max theater a four-story screen shows ecological blockbusters, but it's the new planetarium, a dramatic 87ft (27m) sphere in a glass cube, that takes the cake.

Lincoln Center

HIGHLIGHTS

- Chandeliers in the Met foyer and auditorium
- Reflecting Pool with Henry Moore's *Reclining Figure* (1965)
- Lincoln Center Out-of-Doors Festival
- NY City Ballet's *Nutcracker*
- Chagall murals, Met foyer
- Thursday morning rehearsals, Avery Fisher Hall
- New York Film Festival
- Philip Johnson's Plaza fountain
- Jazz at Lincoln Center
- Annual Messiah singalong

TIP

- Dance under the stars at the Midsummer Night's Swing in Josie Robertson Plaza, a free summertime series of live band sessions.

Strolling to the fantastically fairy-lighted 10-story Metropolitan Opera House colonnade across the Central Plaza on a winter's night is one of the most glamorous things you can do in this city, and you don't need tickets.

West Side Story The Rockefeller-funded über-arts center was envisaged in the late 1950s and finished in 1969, after 7,000 families and 800 businesses had been pushed aside by developer Robert Moses and the John D. Rockefeller millions. Much of *West Side Story* was filmed here after the demolition began.

All the arts The 15 acres (6ha) include megahouses for the biggest-scale arts, all designed by different architects in the same white travertine.

Lincoln Center at night, with one of the Marc Chagall murals visible behind the left-hand arch (left); Christmas decorations add sparkle to the Central Plaza (below)

The Metropolitan Opera House is the glamour queen, with her vast Marc Chagall murals, miles of red carpet, swooshes of stair and starry chandeliers that thrillingly rise to the gold-leaf ceiling before performances. You can take a fascinating back stage tour (weekdays Oct–May, Sunday). Avery Fisher Hall is home to America's oldest orchestra, the NY Philharmonic, while the Juilliard School of Music supplies it with fresh talent. The New York State Theater, housing the New York City Opera and the New York City Ballet, faces Avery Fisher across the Plaza. The Rose Theater is the centerpiece of Jazz at Lincoln Center in the Time Warner Center. Two smaller theaters, the Vivian Beaumont and Mitzi Newhouse, and a more intimate concert hall, Alice Tully, plus the Walter Reade movie theater and the little Bruno Walter Auditorium, complete the pack.

THE BASICS

www.lincolncenter.org
✚ B8
✉ 70 Lincoln Center Plaza
☎ 212/546-2656
Met 212/362-6000
Avery Fisher Hall
212/875-5030
Jazz 212/258-9800
🕐 Inquire for performance times
🍴 Restaurants, cafés, bars
🚇 1 66th Street-Lincoln Center
🚌 M5, M7, M104, crosstown M66
♿ Good
🎫 Admission to Center free
❓ Tours leave from concourse under Met, daily 10.30–4.30 ☎ 212/875-5350 (Lincoln Center), 212/769-7020 (Met)

A Walk on the West Side

The Upper West Side is famous for its grand apartment buildings.

DISTANCE: 1.5 miles (2.5km)   **ALLOW:** 40 minutes

START

END

THE DAKOTA
➕ C7 🚇 B, C 72nd Street

AMERICAN MUSEUM OF NATURAL HISTORY
➕ C6 🚇 B, C 81st Street-Museum of Natural History

① Start at the Dakota on the north-west corner of Central Park West and 72nd Street. John Lennon lived and died here. Cross Central Park West to see the Strawberry Fields memorial.

⑧ Cross 77th Street and you'll have arrived at the American Museum of Natural History. Allow lots of time for your visit here.

② Return to Central Park West and turn left. Walk south to West 65th Street. Turn right and walk west toward Broadway. Cross to Lincoln Center.

⑦ Walk north and you'll pass the San Remo Apartments (former residents include Paul Simon and Dustin Hoffman). Keep on north to the New York Historical Society on the corner of 77th Street. The shop here has interesting gifts.

③ Explore Lincoln Center and its pleasant open-air areas. Then head to the steps of the Juilliard School and turn right, then left onto Broadway. Re-cross Broadway.

⑥ Continue to Amsterdam Avenue and then turn right. Ahead, the Ansonia Building stands between Broadway and W 73rd and 74th streets. Next head right on W 73rd Street back to Central Park West and the Dakota again.

④ Turn left onto Columbus Avenue. Walk north toward 70th Street past the ABC Building. At W 70th Street turn left and head west to 135 W 70th Street.

⑤ Admire the cobalt blue glass of the art deco Pythian Temple, a masonic lodge turned apartment building.

Shopping

APPLAUSE THEATRE AND CINEMA BOOKS

A treasure trove of books on the performing arts from the Broadway stage to the cinema screen.
➕ B7 ✉ 211 W 71st Street/Broadway ☎ 212/496-7511 Ⓜ 1, 2, 3 72nd Street

BARNES AND NOBLE

This is one of the megabook chain's main New York branches. There's usually an evening reading.
➕ B5 ✉ 2289 Broadway/82nd Street ☎ 212/362-8835, and branches Ⓜ 1 79th Street

BETSEY JOHNSON

This long-lived fashion darling produces fun looks.
➕ C7 ✉ 248 Columbus Avenue/71st Street ☎ 212/362-3364 Ⓜ 1, 2, 3, B, C 72nd Street

FAIRWAY

Get a taste of Upper West Side everyday life at this bewilderingly comprehensive grocery.
➕ B7 ✉ 2127 Broadway/75th Street ☎ 212/595-1888 Ⓜ 1, 2, 3 72nd Street

KENNETH COLE

Quality shoes ranging from urban footwear to trendy fashion styles, and simple but stylish clothes for women and men, plus handbags, jewelry, sunglasses and other accessories.
➕ B6 ✉ 353 Columbus Avenue between W 76th and 77th streets ☎ 212/873-2061 Ⓜ 1 79th Street

LAILA ROWE

This is one of a growing chain-ette of accessories stores, crammed with colorful gear. Expect a fun vibe and fast-changing selections of jewelry at prices that belie their on-the-money directional style.
➕ C7 ✉ 253 Columbus Avenue/72nd Street ☎ 212/579-5254 Ⓜ B, C, 1, 2, 3 72nd Street

MALIA MILLS

The boutique swimwear emporium cherished by every woman who's ever loathed her reflection: there are mix-and-match pieces made to fit everyone—and they're super-cool, too.
➕ C7 ✉ 220 Columbus Avenue/70th Street ☎ 212/874-7200 Ⓜ 1, 2, 3, B, C 72nd Street

---

SUMMER IN THE CITY

One of the best reasons to brave the summer heat is for the wonderful selection of free entertainment put on by many of the city's premier cultural institutions. Without paying a dime it's possible to enjoy alfresco operas, theater, art, eating, jazz, classical music, movies, dance, rock-and-roll, blues and folk music. Many arrive early for big performances and stake out a spot for a picnic.

PATAGONIA

If you like social and environmental consciousness with your outdoor wear but still want to look slick while climbing the mountain, swimming the Channel or just look like you might have done so, then this is your place.
➕ C6 ✉ 426 Columbus Avenue/80th Street ☎ 917/441-0011 Ⓜ B, C 81st Street-Museum of Natural History

STEVEN ALAN

The Lower East Side look on the Upper West Side: This is a carefully edited array of the most cutting-edge small hipsters' labels, some of them available nowhere else—including Alan's own.
➕ B5 ✉ 465 Amsterdam Avenue/82nd Street ☎ 212/595-8451 Ⓜ 186th Street

ZABAR'S

This is the pleasantly wise-cracking New Yawker of the foodie havens with a Jewish soul all its own. Cheese, coffee, smoked fish and the like are downstairs, while upstairs are the city's best buys in kitchenwares.
➕ B6 ✉ 2245 Broadway/80th Street ☎ 212/787-2000 Ⓜ 1 79th Street

Entertainment and Nightlife

AVERY FISHER HALL
The home of the New York Philharmonic seats 2,700. The hall is also home to other groups including the American Symphony Orchestra.
✚ B8 ✉ 10 Lincoln Center Plaza, Columbus Avenue/65th Street ☎ 212/875-5030 or 212/721-6500 🚇 1 66th Street-Lincoln Center

BEACON THEATRE
Storytelling, readings, children's performance, music, dance and more.
✚ B7 ✉ 2124 Broadway/74th Street ☎ 212/465-6500 🚇 1, 2, 3 72nd Street

BRUNO WALTER AUDITORIUM
Seminars, lectures, films and concerts.
✚ B8 ✉ The New York Library for the Performing Arts, 111 Amsterdam Avenue between 64th and 65th streets ☎ 212/870-1630 or 212/642-0142 🚇 1 66th Street-Lincoln Center

CATHEDRAL CHURCH OF ST. JOHN THE DIVINE
Although the cathedral is still under construction, it stages a range of arts events, such as classical cantatas, jazz, folk music or chanting Tibetan monks.
✚ B1 ✉ 1047 Amsterdam Avenue/112th Street ☎ 212/316-7540 🚇 1 Cathedral Parkway/110th Street

DIZZY'S CLUB COCA COLA
Jazz at Lincoln Center's intimate club is, in the spirit of Dizzy (Gillespie—who else?), designed to make performers and spectators alike *relaaaaax*. The Monday night "Upstarts" series is popular; there are also After Hours sets Tuesday through Saturday nights.
✚ C9 ✉ Time Warner Center at Broadway/60th Street, 5th floor ☎ 212/258-9595 🚇 A, B, C, D, 1 59th Street-Columbus Circle

LINCOLN PLAZA CINEMAS
Six screens showing successful first runs and foreign movies.
✚ B8 ✉ 1886 Broadway/63rd Street ☎ 212/757-2280 🚇 1 66th Street-Lincoln Center

THE METROPOLITAN OPERA
The gala openings at this world-class opera rank among the most glamorous of the city's cultural events. Serious buffs line up on Saturday mornings for inexpensive standing-room tickets. The season runs October to April.
✚ B8 ✉ 30 Lincoln Center ☎ 212/362-6000 🚇 1 66th Street-Lincoln Center

NEW YORK CITY OPERA
The repertoire of this fine opera company, the Met's neighbor, incorporates a wider variety including newer works, operetta and musicals.
✚ B8 ✉ New York State Theater, Lincoln Center ☎ 212/870-5570 🚇 1 66th Street-Lincoln Center

SMOKE
Plush couches adorn this intimate lounge, which hosts great jazz artists and local favorites.
✚ B2 ✉ 2751 Broadway/105th Street ☎ 212/864-6662 🚇 1 103rd Street

STAND UP NEW YORK
Traditional comedy club where new and aspiring comics test their routines.
✚ B6 ✉ 236 W 78th Street/Broadway ☎ 212/595-0850 🚇 1 79th Street

SYMPHONY SPACE
Storytelling, readings, children's theater, music, film, dance and more.
✚ B4 ✉ 2537 Broadway/95th Street ☎ 212/864-5400 🚇 1, 2, 3 96th Street

---

BIG IN NEW YORK
From the elegance of a grand opera to the excitement of avant-garde performance art, New York spectacles are world-class (even the flops). Broadway shows can be expensive, but nothing transports like a great multi-million-dollar musical or an intense performance by a drama diva. Be sure to reserve tickets in advance for the most popular shows.

ENTERTAINMENT AND NIGHTLIFE

Restaurants

PRICES

Prices are approximate, based on a 3-course meal for one person.
$$$	over $60
$$	$40–$60
$	under $40

AIX ($$$)

Didier Virot has brought his own style of robust Provençal cuisine to the Upper West Side at this tri-level restaurant that's always busy. Thyme-citrus smoked brisket and crispy *dorade* with Parmesan crust are typical dishes.

➕ B5 ✉ 2398 Broadway/88th Street ☎ 212/874-7400 🕐 Closed lunch 🚇 1 86th Street

BARNEY GREENGRASS ($)

An Upper West Side tradition since 1929, this is frantic on weekends, when locals feast on huge platters of smoked fish—whitefish, sable, sturgeon and lox—or sandwiches made with similar contents.

➕ B5 ✉ 541 Amsterdam Avenue/86th Street ☎ 212/724-4707 🕐 Closed Mon 🚇 1 86th Street

BOAT BASIN CAFÉ ($)

It's hard to find this totally unpretentious place practically on the banks of the Hudson, but if you do, it's worth waiting for a terrace table. The food is dinerlike, but you'll be dazzled by the view.

➕ A6 ✉ W 79th Street/Hudson River ☎ 212/496-5542 🚇 1 79th Street

CAFÉ DES ARTISTES ($$)

Howard Chandler Christy murals of frolicking nude nymphs adorn this romantic, art nouveau dining room. The menu is an appealing mix of Hungarian and French dishes, from sturgeon schnitzel to pot au feu.

➕ C8 ✉ 1 W 67th Street/Central Park West–Columbus Avenue ☎ 212/877-3500 🕐 Closed Mon–Fri lunch 🚇 1 66th Street-Lincoln Center

CARMINE'S ($–$$)

Join the mob scene here—no, it's not actually anything to do with the Mafia, but this beloved, raucous place does serve its Sicilian-Italian dishes family-style—huge platters to share. It's not for picky foodies, but it's fun.

➕ B4 ✉ 2450 Broadway/90th Street ☎ 212/362-2200 🚇 1, 2 96th Street

BRUNCH

It's hard to imagine what New Yorkers did before the invention of brunch. These days the weekend noontime meal can be everything from the basic omelet to a multi-course culinary adventure and it certainly needn't be consumed before noon. A 2pm brunch with mimosas is just fine.

JEAN-GEORGES ($$–$$$)

One of the world's—let alone New York's—great chefs, Alsace native Jean Georges Vongerichten's refined, full-flavored Asian-accented style cannot be imitated. The glass-walled minimalist rooms feel serene and special—perhaps because they were Feng-Shui-ed? Don't miss the molten-center chocolate cake.

➕ C9 ✉ 1 Central Park West ☎ 212/299-3900 🕐 Closed Sat lunch, Sun 🚇 A, C, 1, B, D 59th Street-Columbus Circle

OUEST ($$–$$$)

This place single-handedly revitalized the moribund Upper West Side dining scene—with its red booths and the inspired Euro-American posh comfort dishes of chef Tom Valenti. His lamb shanks are legendary.

➕ B5 ✉ 2315 Broadway/83rd Street ☎ 212/580-8700 🚇 1 86th Street

PICHOLINE ($$$)

The Mediterranean cuisine of Terrance Brennan is as good as it ever was at his first New York address. Though everybody has got into the cheese act now, this is still the best cart in town (except Artisanal).

➕ C8 ✉ 35 W 64th Street between Central Park West and Broadway ☎ 212/724-8585 🕐 Closed lunch 🚇 1 66th Street-Lincoln Center

Farther Afield

New York extends far beyond Manhattan and its outer boroughs are increasingly attractive to those who seek a more relaxed approach to life. Brooklyn especially has plenty to engage visitors.

Brooklyn

Brooklyn has it all—one of the largest art museums in the US and some of New York's best restaurants; beaches and a park; a zoo, aquarium and children's museum; hip neighborhoods and avant-garde arts.

Big, bigger, biggest If Brooklyn were still a separate city, it would be the fourth largest in the US. Home to more than 2 million people, it is the most populous of New York's boroughs and the most diverse, with Russian, Middle Eastern, Italian, West Indian, Hasidic Jewish and Chinese neighborhoods. The Brooklyn Museum of Art, intended by McKim, Mead & White to be the biggest museum in the world (it's actually the seventh largest in the US), has collections ranging from pre-Columbian art to 58 Rodin sculptures, plus what many feel

Remsen Street in Brooklyn Heights (left); Brooklyn Bridge seen from Seaport Pier, Manhattan (below)

are the best Egyptian rooms outside the British Museum (and Egypt). With its grand new entrance (opened summer 2004), it abuts Prospect Park—opened in 1867. The Botanic Garden, zoo and the Bandshell summertime events are highlights.

The bridge and beyond With its twin Gothic towers and ballet of cables, the first Manhattan–Brooklyn link fulfills beautifully its symbolic role of affording entry into new worlds of opportunity and the view from here is spectacular. Worth exploring are the established brownstone neighborhoods of Park Slope, Cobble Hill and Brooklyn Heights, the latter famous for the Promenade and its view of Manhattan. Brooklyn Children's Museum, the world's first for kids, has tons to do, including a miniature theater and the "Totally Tots" toddler stamping ground.

THE BASICS

Brooklyn Heights
H22
2, 3 Clark Street

Brooklyn Museum of Art
Off map to southeast
200 Eastern Parkway
718/638-5000
Wed–Fri 10–5, Sat–Sun 11–6
2, 3, Eastern Parkway-Brooklyn Museum

Prospect Park
Off map to southeast
718/965-8999
2, 3 Eastern Parkway-Brooklyn Museum

Brooklyn Children's Museum
www.brooklynkids.org
Off map to southeast
145 Brooklyn Avenue, Crown Heights
718/735-4400
Wed–Fri 1–6 (12– 6 Jul–Aug), Sat–Sun 11–6
C Kingston-Throop avenues
Moderate

More to See

BRONX ZOO

The biggest city zoo in the US, 100 years old in 1999, has 4,000 animals, a kid's zoo and monorail. Don't miss the $43 million Congo Gorilla Forest.
🚼 Off map to northeast ✉ Fordham Road (Bronx River Parkway Northeast) ☎ 718/367-1010 🕐 Apr–end Oct daily 10–5; Nov–end Mar 10–4.30 🍴 Restaurant 🚇 2, 5 Pelham Parkway 💰 Expensive

THE CLOISTERS

A 12th-century Spanish apse attached to a Romanesque cloister and a Gothic chapel—what's all this doing in the Bronx? This is the Met's medieval branch: The incongruity is hallucinogenic and the sights are just heavenly. The collections are arranged chronologically, so you can trace the metamorphosis of architectural styles. The bulk of the art and architecture was amassed by sculptor George Gray Bernard in the early 20th century. Much was rescued from ruin: The effigy of the Crusader Jean d'Alluye, for instance, was doing duty as a bridge, while the priceless Unicorn Tapestries were acting as frost blankets.
🚼 Off map to north ✉ Fort Tryon Park, North Manhattan ☎ 212/923-3700 🕐 Mar–end Oct Tue–Sun 9.30–5.15; Nov–end Feb Tue–Sun 9.30–4.45. Closed holidays 🚇 A 190th Street 💰 Expensive

CONEY ISLAND

At the end of the 19th century, Coney Island on a peak day played host to a million people. By 1921 a boardwalk and the subway had arrived, then 1939–40 added the "Parachute Jump," now a rusted ghost. The glory days of Luna Park are long since gone, yet seedy Coney Island still draws a crowd. The big-dipper ride, the Cyclone, is still there and Nathan's Famous hot dogs are still sold from the original site. A newer attraction is KeySpan Park, home of the Brookyn Cyclones baseball team. Look out for concerts held here in summer. The New York Aquarium, watery branch of the Bronx Zoo, moved here in 1957. Roughly 10,000 creatures call it home, including beluga whales, coral,

The restful garden at The Cloisters

A Kodiak bear at Bronx Zoo

a penguin colony and sharks.
➕ Off map to south ✉ Surf Avenue, Boardwalk; Aquarium: W 8th Street, Surf Avenue ☎ Sideshow 718/372-5159; KeySpan Park 718/449-8497; Aquarium 718/265-3474 🕐 Aquarium daily 10–5, summer weekends and holidays 10–7 🍴 Cafeteria at Aquarium 🚇 D, F, N Q Coney Island-Stillwell Avenue 💰 Aquarium expensive

QUEENS
The major attractions here are the New York Hall of Science and Queens Museum of Art. The former is a hands-on science and technology museum with a wonderful Science Playground outside for children (✉ 111th Street, Flushing Meadows-Corona Park ☎ 718/699-0005). The art museum (New York Building, Flushing Meadows-Corona Park ☎ 718/592-9700) holds exhibitions of contemporary art, Tiffany glassware and a scale panorama of New York that is regularly updated. Outside stands the Unisphere—the world's largest globe.
➕ Off map to east

STATEN ISLAND
Fine historic sights are housed here. The Alice Austen House (✉ 2 Hylan Boulevard ☎ 718/816-4506) is a museum of photographs by Alice Austen in her Victorian house.

Historic Richmond Town (✉ 441 Clarke Avenue ☎ 718/351-1611) is a restored rural village re-creating the early 19th century.
➕ Off map to southwest

YANKEE STADIUM
If you want to see what makes the New Yorker tick, go see a Yankees home game. The Yankees dominated the early era of baseball. In 1920 Babe Ruth joined the team and quickly became a hero. The team had an incredible winning streak when they clinched the World Series title in 1996, 1998, 1999, and 2000.
➕ Off map to north ✉ E 161st Street, Bronx ☎ 718/293-6000, Ticketmaster 212/307-1212 🕐 Season runs Apr–end Oct. Check schedule for games 🍴 Concession stands 🚇 4, B, D 161st Street-Yankee Stadium 💰 Expensive

Shea Stadium, Queens

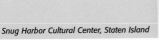

Snug Harbor Cultural Center, Staten Island

Restauants

RESTAURANTS

FARTHER AFIELD

PRICES

Prices are approximate, based on a 3-course meal for one person.

$$$	over $60
$$	$40–$60
$	under $40

AL DI LA ($$)

One of the first food-forward serious restaurants in Brooklyn is still one of the best, as you'll notice as you stand in line (no reservations) or wait in the adjunct wine bar. The food is hearty and Venetian; the look is flea-market chic.
✉ 248 5th Avenue/Carroll Street, Brooklyn ☎ 718/783-4565 🚇 M, N, R Union Street

BLUE RIBBON ($$)

There's quite a Manhattan feel to this deceptively huge modern-American foodies' favorite, and that's not surprising since it has an older sister there (97 Sullivan Street/Prince Street, 212/274-0404), beloved by off-duty chefs. The comprehensive menu is perfectly balanced between creativity and comfort.
✉ 280 5th Avenue/1st Street, Brooklyn ☎ 718/840-0404 🚇 M, R Union Street

BUBBY'S ($)

The DUMBO branch of this Tribeca favorite has an identical kitchen serving all-American BLTs, chicken clubs, meat loaf and fries followed by its divine pies but the rest differs enormously—operative word "enormous." Despite its size, expect a stroller jam and a wait at the door for Sunday brunch.
✉ 1 Main Street/Water Street, Brooklyn ☎ 718/222-0666 🚇 F York Street

GROCERY ($$$)

A tiny place with a big reputation, this sweet Carroll Gardens chef-owned place offers constantly changing market-led nouvelle-American menus. Inside is homey, but the lovely tree-shaded garden takes the cake.
✉ 288 Smith Street/Sacket, Brooklyn ☎ 718/596-3335 🚇 F, G Carroll Street

JUNIOR'S ($)

An institution in a hideous stretch of downtown Brooklyn, this

SHERWOOD CAFÉ

It started out just selling funky French antiques, but the adjunct café grew until it took over entirely. One of the places that kicked the Brooklyn boom into high gear, the place is always packed, for the good French bistro food, the wacky interior and the fairy-tale graveled garden.
✉ 195 Smith Street/Baltic Street, Brooklyn ☎ 718/596-1609 🚇 F, G Bergen Street

two-room diner (the "Café" in the back is quieter) is famous for its twin, two-roll, sandwiches and huge portions but, above all, for its creamy, classic New York cheesecake.
✉ 386 Flatbush Avenue/DeKalb Avenue, Brooklyn ☎ 718/852-5257 🚇 B, M, Q, R DeKalb Avenue

OSAKA ($$)

Often cited as one of New York's, let alone Brooklyn's, best sushi places, this trendy hole-in-the-wall has some creative maki and salads and a cute wooden-decked garden that more than doubles its size the warm months.
✉ 272 Court Street/Degraw, Brooklyn ☎ 718/643-0044 🚇 F, G Bergen Street

PETER LUGER ($$$)

You get steak, some hash browns and creamed spinach for the table, and maybe some tomato-and-onion salad to start—that's it, and that's all you need. It's not about atmosphere or fine wines, it's not about feeling special, it's about steak. Since 1887 this landmark has been serving the best beef in New York.
✉ 178 Broadway/Driggs Avenue, Brooklyn ☎ 718/387-7400; no credit cards 🚇 J, M, Z Marcy Avenue

Where to Stay

Like all major cities, New York has a range of accommodations from ultratrendy and extravagantly plush to inexpensive B&Bs and chain hotels, with plenty in between.

Staying in New York

There are plenty of hotel rooms but it is hard to find a comfortable room under $150. If money is no object, reserve a room at the Four Seasons.

On a Budget

For less expensive options, check out the inexpensive chains—Red Roof, Super 8 and others. The city also has some B&Bs, less expensive than the average hotel, with good-value extras. Hostels are the least expensive lodging options (see the box below).

Luxury Living

You'll find first-class luxury hotels spread throughout the city, although many are centered in Midtown. Nearly every hotel room comes with air-conditioning, private bathroom, cable TV, telephone, coffeemaker, hand hair dryer, but top-class hotel rooms boast luxe fabrics and linens, high-tech electronics, and high staff-to-guest ratios.

Prices

Today there is no such thing as a standard rack rate. Prices fluctuate with customer demand. To get the best rate on a hotel room, call the hotel and ask about the best available rate and special discounts. Alternatively, go online to such discount services as hotels.com, quikbook.com or hoteldiscounts.com. Note that taxes will be added to your bill, plus $2 occupancy tax on a standard room and 5 percent of the bill.

HOSTELS IN NEW YORK

Big Apple Hostel 119 W 45th, tel 212/302-2603.
Chelsea Center Hostel 313 W 29th Street, 10031, tel 212/643-0214.
Chelsea International Hostel 251 W 20th Street, tel 212/647-0010.
Hostelling International 891 Amsterdam Avenue, tel 212/932-2300.
West Side YMCA 5 W 63rd Street, tel 212/630-9600.
Whitehouse 340 Bowery, tel 212/477-5623.

Top to bottom: arriving at the hotel; Peninsula Hotel; doorman at the Ritz-Carlton; Bryant Park hotel

Budget Hotels

PRICES

Expect to pay between $80 and $200 for a budget hotel

CARLTON ARMS

www.carltonarms.com
Decorated with crazy murals, this is perhaps New York's wackiest hotel. Amenities are minimal but there is a communal atmosphere that makes travelers feel at home. As it says on the business card, "this ain't no Holiday Inn." 54 rooms.

🔲 F14 ✉ 160 E 25th Street/Lexington–3rd avenues ☎ 212/684-8337 🚇 6 23rd Street

GERSHWIN

www.gershwinhotel.com
"We're just at the edge of hip," says the manager of this first New York Interclub hotel—Urs Jakob's string of super-hostels. Art elevates the style of the 150 basic rooms; bars, roofdecks and lounges encourage sociability.

🔲 E13 ✉ 7 E 27th Street/5th–Madison avenues ☎ 212/545-8000 🍴 Café 🚇 N, R, W 23rd Street

HOTEL BELLECLAIRE

www.hotelbelleclaire.com
Mark Twain lived here, as did Maxim Gorky. Now the early-20th-century building offers 167 clean, minimal guest rooms, with pine furniture and pale apricot-color walls

though only the shared-bathroom rooms are budget rate.

🔲 B6 ✉ 250 W 77th Street/Broadway–11th Avenue ☎ 212/362-7700; fax: 212/362-1004 🚇 1 79th Street

HOTEL 17

www.hotel17ny.com
The kitschy decor almost looks deliberate—its stripey wallpaper, floral bedspread, nylon carpet look seems to hit a chord with rock and roll types and models. That could also be on account of its brownstone New York Gramercy Park location and its dirt cheap rates. Shared and private baths.

🔲 F15 ✉ 225 E 17th Street/2nd–3rd avenues ☎ 212/475-2845 🚇 L 3rd Avenue

HOTEL QT

www.hotelqt.com
Hot hotelier Andre Balazs's first budget hotel

B&BS

Those who prefer real neighborhoods, authentic experiences and behaving like a local may opt for a B&B. Often these are found in Brooklyn brownstones, where the host has an extra room. Others are empty apartments. The only imperative is to reserve ahead. Another ever-more-popular option is to check the sublet vacation rentals and housing swap listings at www.craigslist.org

offers no-frills rooms with bunk beds and smart, minimalist decor: the off-lobby exhibitionists' swimming pool and other high-design features are mostly found in the public areas. Rooms have nice bed-linens, flatscreen TVs and Wi-Fi. It's meant for—and attracts—the young.

🔲 D11 ✉ 125 W 45th Street/6th–7th avenues ☎ 212/354-2323 🚇 B, D, F, V 42nd Street-Bryant Park

HOTEL WOLCOTT

www.wolcott.com
Within walking distance of Macy's, the Empire State Building and other attractions, this hotel is great value for money. It has comfortable rooms with private bath and even offers free morning coffee and muffins.

🔲 D13 ✉ 4 W 31st Street between 5th Avenue and Broadway ☎ 212/268-2900 🚇 B, D, F, N, Q, R, V, W, 34th Street-Herald Square

WASHINGTON SQUARE

www.washingtonsquarehotel.com
This is the only hotel in the heart of Greenwich Village. Amenities are minimal—deliberately so, to keep the rates down—but the place still manages to be almost chic. 165 rooms.

🔲 E16 ✉ 103 Waverley Place/MacDougal Street ☎ 212/777-9515 🍴 CIII 🚇 A, C, E, B, D, F, V, W 4th Street-Washington Square

Mid-Range Hotels

PRICES

Expect to pay between $200 and $400 for a mid-range hotel

BEEKMAN TOWER

www.thebeekmanhotel.com
The art deco tower in far-east Midtown has a lot going for it: well-kept rooms and suites, some with kitchens, most larger than the average but somewhat fusty but comfy furnishings, a fitness center, room service and two restaurants including the 26th-story Top of the Tower, with great river and city views.
G10 3 Mitchell Place/1st Avenue 212/355-7300 6 51st Street

THE BENJAMIN

www.thebenjamin.com
Rooms in this environmentally conscious Midtown 1920s block have a sophisticated neutral palette, excellent work areas with printer/faxes and beds with Frette sheets, down duvets and pillows. Caring service, plus a spa, fitness center, room service, restaurant and wine bar all add up to an excellent value.
E10 125 E 50th Street/Park Avenue 212/715-2500 6 51st Street

CHELSEA HOTEL

www.hotelchelsea.com
Half of this Chelsea landmark houses residents of the louche, trendsetting, artistic kind. The rest of the rooms appeal to visitors who value the hotel's rock-and-roll history, art-lined corridors and shabby chic decor. Room sizes vary—the small ones are pretty basic—and housekeeping is hit or miss. But the faded grandeur may soon be a thing of the past, as a new management company may bring changes. If you want to experience this legendary dive, better make it quick.
C14 222 W 23rd Street/7th Avenue 212/243-3700 1 23rd Street

COSMOPOLITAN

www.cosmohotel.com
No frills in any sense of the word exist at this 125-room, seven-story block in Tribeca. But, if you find the real estate rule applies to hotels, you'll love it—the location, location, location is prime. The clean, fully functional rooms vary a good deal in size, so if they're not full and you're not happy, ask to see another.
E20 95 W Broadway/Chambers Street 212/566-1900 A, C Chambers Street

EXCELSIOR

www.excelsiorhotelny.com
The location is quite fabulous, steps from Central Park and the American Museum of Natural History, with the subway practically underfoot. The building is grand, too, heavy on the wood paneling, faux-oils and gilt frames. Rooms, though not beautiful in the generic brocades and stripes, are fine; some standard ones even overlook the park.
C6 45 W 81st Street/Central Park West 212/362-9200 B, C 81st Street-Museum of Natural History

HOTEL BEACON

www.beaconhotel.com
In the middle of Broadway, on the Upper West Side, the Beacon feels more like an apartment building than a hotel. Some of the 200-plus rooms have kitchenettes.
B7 2130 Broadway/75th Street 212/787-1100 1, 2, 3 72nd Street

MARITIME HOTEL

www.themaritimehotel.com
Heat-seeking trendsters will love this quirky 120-room place in the thick of the Meatpacking District. Porthole windows facing the Hudson conceal small rooms with a shiplike feel and navy-blue soft furnishings. Fitness center, happening bar scene and Japanese restaurant.
🞣 C15 ✉ 363 W 16th Street/9th Avenue ☎ 212/242-4300 🍴 Matsuri 🚇 A, C, E 14th Street

OFF SOHO SUITES

www.offsoho.com
Since this place opened a few years ago, its very off-SoHo location on the Lower East Side bordering Nolita has become all the rage. The suites are mini-studio apartments with no decorative advantages whatsoever but with full kitchens, private phones and satellite TV. "Economy" suites share kitchen and bathroom.
🞣 F18 ✉ 11 Rivington Street/Bowery ☎ 212/979-9808 🚇 F Lower East Side-2nd Avenue; J, M, Z Bowery

70 PARK AVENUE

www.70parkave.com
The first foray into New York by boutique hotel pioneers Kimpton, this 205-room Murray Hill place has a quietly contemporary decor, extras like touch-screen room service, pillow menu, good sound systems and a special yoga channel on the huge flatscreen TV.
🞣 E12 ✉ 70 Park Avenue/38th Street ☎ 212/973-2400 🍴 Silverleaf Tavern 🚇 4, 5, 6, 7, S Grand Central Station 42nd Street

THE SALISBURY

www.nycsalisbury.com
Across from Carnegie Hall and a short walk to Central Park and Fifth Avenue shopping, the Salisbury is comfortable in price as well as accommodations. The 119 rooms and 85 suites are large and quiet and most have refrigerators and serving pantries.
🞣 D9 ✉ 123 W 57th Street between 6th and 7th avenues ☎ 212/246-1300 🚇 N, Q, R, W 57th Street-7th Avenue; F 57th Street

THE SHOREHAM

www.shorehamhotel.com
The sleek Shoreham

Hotel, behind the Museum of Modern Art, has 174 small but nice rooms and suites, with ultra-suede walls, diffused lighting and puffy white comforters on the beds. The choice rooms are in the back. Extras such as Aveda products, free round-the-clock cappuccino and espresso and a hotel-curated art gallery, plus high-end electronics (Bose Wave, plasma screens, XBox 360s) in the better rooms add value.
🞣 D10 ✉ 33 W 55th Street/5th–6th avenues ☎ 212/247-6700 🍴 La Caravelle 🚇 B, Q 57th Street

THE TIME

www.thetimeny.com
Just off Times Square, the 164 rooms and 28 suites sport bold, primary colors. Choose a red, yellow or blue room and you'll find that color not only covering the bed and selected wall parts but also appearing in candy and scent form. A Bose radio and Molton Brown toiletries add value but can't make the small rooms grow any larger, though you can spread out a bit in the small gym and rather swank lounge and restaurant.
🞣 C11 ✉ 224 W 49th Street/8th Avenue ☎ 212/246-5252 🚇 N, Q, R, S, W, 1, 2, 3, 7 Times Square-42nd Street

Luxury Hotels

PRICES

Expect to pay from $400 for a luxury hotel

FOUR SEASONS

www.fourseasons.com

The grandiose I. M. Pei building makes a big first impression—all towering lobbies, marble and mezzanine lounges. And the rooms don't disappoint. In beiges and creams, they're big, with tons of closets, tubs that fill in no time and, in some, great views. Many consider this Manhattan's top hotel.

E9 ✉ 57 E 57th Street, Park–Madison avenues ☎ 212/758-5700 🍴 57, L'Atelier de Joël Robuchon 🚇 F, Q 57th Street

HOTEL GANSEVOORT

www.hotelgansevoort.com

You see the illuminated glass tower for blocks. Fashion-obsessed young creatives consider this area style-central and populate the stark rooms with their stone and sand colors and high-tech everything, and the popular Ono restaurant and its O Bar. The rooftop pool is a treat.

🏨 C16 ✉ 18 9th Avenue/ 13th Street ☎ 212/206-6700 🚇 A, C, E 14th Street; L 8th Avenue

INN AT IRVING PLACE

www.innatirving.com

With just 12 guest rooms and junior suites, this discreet hotel is set in two 1830s townhouses near Gramercy Park, with elegant decor and a romantic atmosphere.

🏨 E15 ✉ 56 Irving Place ☎ 212/533-4600 🍴 Dining: Casa Mono 🚇 4, 5, 6, L, N, Q, R, W 14th Street-Union Square

MANDARIN ORIENTAL

www.mandarinoriental.com

This chain is known for its clean lines, its fabulous spas and its service. The best of the 248 rooms and suites have panoramic views.

🏨 C9 ✉ 80 Columbus Circle/60th Street ☎ 212/805-8800 🍴 Asiate 🚇 A, B, C, D, 1 59th Street-Columbus Circle

MERCER HOTEL

www.mercerhotel.com

In André Balazs' hip hotel, in central SoHo, the Christian Liaigre design is cool and calm. The rooms are huge (mostly)

THE STYLE OF LUXURY

In the last two decades a crop of ultrachic hotels have opened around the city that offer guests truly luxurious amenities in modern, stylish settings. The first was the Royalton, which started the trend in 1987. A steady trickle followed…then the deluge. The hotels not only offer hip accommodations and grand services, but also restaurants, lounges and bars that attract trendy New Yorkers from all corners of the city.

and sexy; the lobby, bar and basement restaurant attract locals and visitors.

🏨 E18 ✉ 147 Mercer Street/Prince Street ☎ 212/ 966-6060 🍴 Mercer Kitchen 🚇 N, R, W Prince Street

RITZ-CARLTON BATTERY PARK

www.ritzcarlton.com

This glass-sided tower has one thing no other hotel has: the harbor. Decor in the rooms-with-everything is pale and contemporary, and the service and facilities are exemplary.

🏨 D23 ✉ 2 West Street/ Battery Place ☎ 212/344-0800 🚇 1 South Ferry

ST. REGIS

www.stregis.com

Formal Louis XV style in the middle of Midtown. The service is discreet, and the 182 rooms and suites are plush.

🏨 E9–E10 ✉ 2 E 55th Street/5th Avenue ☎ 212/753-4500 🚇 E, V 5th Avenue-53rd Street

60 THOMPSON

www.60thompson.com

Fashionista boutique hotel in SoHo with 100 contemporary rooms. Most bathrooms have only showers. The rooftop bar/lounge, A60, is ever so glamorous, as is the Thai restaurant, Kittichai, and the bar, Thom.

🏨 D18 ✉ 60 Thompson Street/Broome ☎ 877/431-0400 🚇 A, C, E Canal Street

Use this section to help you plan your visit to New York. We have suggested the best ways to get around the city and useful information for while you are there.

Planning Ahead

When to Go

Fall is generally thought the best time to visit New York. In August many New Yorkers are driven out of town by the searing heat. However, during this time lines are shorter, restaurant reservations optional and outdoor festivals at their peak. The city has occasional blizzards in winter, but these rarely cause disruption.

TIME

New York is on Eastern Standard Time, three hours ahead of Los Angeles and five hours behind the UK.

AVERAGE DAILY MAXIMUM TEMPERATURES											
JAN	FEB	MAR	APR	MAY	JUN	JUL	AUG	SEP	OCT	NOV	DEC
39°F	41°F	46°F	61°F	70°F	81°F	84°F	82°F	77°F	66°F	54°F	39°F
4°C	5°C	8°C	16°C	21°C	27°C	29°C	28°C	25°C	19°C	12°C	4°C

Spring (March to May) is unpredictable—even in April snow showers can alternate with shirtsleeves weather—but the worst of winter is over by mid-March.
Summer (June to August) can be extremely hot and humid, especially July and August.
Fall (September to November) sees warm temperatures persisting into October.
Winter (December to February) can be severe, with heavy snow, biting winds and subfreezing temperatures.

WHAT'S ON

January/February *Chinese New Year* (Chinatown).
Martin Luther King Day Parade (3rd Mon in Jan, 5th Avenue, 61st–86th streets).
March 17 *St. Patrick's Day Parade* (5th Avenue, 44th–86th streets).
March/April *Easter Parade* (5th Avenue, 44th–59th streets).
April–October *Baseball*
May *9th Avenue International Food Festival* (9th Avenue, 37th–57th streets ☎ 800/894-9166).
June *Metropolitan Opera park concerts* (☎ 212/362-6000).
JVC Jazz Festival (various

venues; www.festivalnetwork.com).
Lesbian and Gay Pride Parade (5th Avenue, Midtown to Washington Square).
July 4 *Independence Day*
July–August *Shakespeare in the Park* (Delacorte Theater ☎ 212/539-8665).
NY Philharmonic park concerts (☎ 212/875-5709).
August *Harlem Week* (☎ 212/862-8477).
August–September *Lincoln Center Out-of-Doors Festival* (☎ 212/546-2656).
US Open Tennis Championships (☎ 718/760-6200).

September *Feast of San Gennaro* (Little Italy).
September–October *New York Film Festival* (Lincoln Center ☎ 212/875-5600).
Columbus Day Parade (5th Avenue, 44th–79th streets).
November *NYC Marathon* (Staten Island to Central Park ☎ 212/860-4455).
Macy's Thanksgiving Day Parade (✉ Central Park West, 81st Street ☎ 212/484-1222).
December *Tree Lighting Ceremony* (✉ Rockefeller Center ☎ 212/332-6868).
New Year's Eve celebrations (✉ Times Square).

New York City Online

www.livebroadway.com
Live Broadway offers up-to-the-minute details on show times and tickets, as well as reviews.

http://newyork.citysearch.com
City Search has links to and listings for attractions, entertainment, restaurants, shopping, hotels and more. Also has news, reviews and a directory offering NYC information.

www.nyc.gov
As the official homepage of the City of New York, the site offers links to the Office of the Mayor as well as information about community services, legal policies, city agencies, news and weather and visitor information.

www.ny.com
Billing itself as "the paperless guide to New York City," ny.com's "How, Wow and Now" sections let you know what's up on New York's entertainment, dining and nightlife scene. The sports section lists professional events.

www.nysale.com
Information on sample sales, showroom sales, warehouse sales and clearance sales.

www.nytimes.com
Here you'll get an inside look at one of the world's most respected newspapers. The site has links to sections covering everything from world affairs to sports and local gossip.

www.nycvisit.com
The official tourism website includes a calendar of events, accommodations information, updates on laws, transit and lots more.

www.timessquare.com
All about Times Square and the area around, Broadway and its theaters in particular, with booking information.

PRIME TRAVEL SITES

www.fodors.com
A complete travel-planning site. You can research prices and weather; book air tickets, cars and rooms; pose questions to fellow travelers and find links to other sites.

www.iloveny.com
Official NY State site. Information about touring the region.

www.mta.info
The Metropolitan Transportation Authority updates you on service changes and disruptions, and answers questions about buses and subway.

INTERNET CAFÉS

Cybercafé
✉ 250 W 49th Street (Broadway/8th Avenue)
☎ 212/333-4109
◉ Mon–Fri 8am–11pm, Sat and Sun 1–11

Kinko's have locations throughout the city, many open 24 hours.

Starbucks now provide wireless hookups, a service that is proliferating in the city.

Getting There

ENTRY REQUIREMENTS

Visitors to New York from outside the US must have a full passport and a return ticket. For countries participating in the Visa Waiver Program, a visa is not required, though you must fill out the green visa-waiver form issued on the plane. You are also required to fill out a customs form and an immigration form.

FROM LAGUARDIA

The journey to Manhattan takes between 45 and 60 minutes. SuperShuttle runs a shared minibus 24 hours (cost $15–$20). Services to Manhattan are also provided by New York Airport Service Express (cost $12–$27). Taxis cost $25–$45, plus tolls and tip.

ARRIVING BY LAND

● Greyhound buses from across the US and Canada and commuter buses from New Jersey arrive at the Port Authority Terminal (✉ 42nd Street/8th Avenue ☎ 212/564-8484).

● Commuter trains use Grand Central Terminal (✉ 42nd Street/Park Avenue ☎ 212/532-4900).

● Long-distance trains arrive at Pennsylvania Station (✉ 31st Street/8th Avenue).

AIRPORTS

New York has three airports—John F. Kennedy (J.F.K.) (✉ Queens, 15 miles/24km east of Manhattan ☎ 718/244-4444), Newark (✉ New Jersey, 16 miles/25km west ☎ 973/961-6000) and LaGuardia (✉ Queens, 8 miles/13km east ☎ 718/533-3400). Most international flights arrive at J.F.K. For details, visit www.panynj.gov

18 MILES (29KM)

Manhattan

LaGuardia Airport
8 miles (13km) to city center. Bus/minibus 45–60 minutes, $12–$21

Newark Liberty International Airport
16 miles (25km) to city center. Bus/minibus 40 minutes, $14–$25

J.F.K. International Airport
15 miles (24km) to city center. Bus/minibus 1 hour, $15–$33

FROM J.F.K.

The journey to Manhattan takes around an hour. New York Airport Service Express Bus (☎ 718/875-8200) runs every 15–30 minutes, 6.15am–11.10pm ($15). The SuperShuttle (☎ 800/451-0455) runs to Manhattan 24 hours a day ($17–$22). To reserve, use the courtesy telephone next to the Ground Transportation Desk. A free shuttle bus runs to the A train. Taxis costs $45 plus tolls; use the official taxi stand. The AirTrain to Jamaica (E.J.Z. subway and Long Island Railroad) or Howard Beach (A subway) costs $5 and takes 12 minutes, plus 60–90 minutes to Midtown.

FROM NEWARK

It takes about 60 minutes to Manhattan. AirTrain (☎ 888/397-4636) goes direct from all terminals to Penn Station (A, C, E, 1, 2, 3 subway); follow signs to Monorail/AirTrain. SuperShuttle (☎ 212/315-3006) runs a minibus to Midtown 7am–11pm ($15–$20). A taxi costs $40–$75, plus tolls and a $15 surcharge from Manhattan.

Getting Around

BUSES

● Bus stops are on or near corners, marked by a sign and a yellow painted curb. Any ride costs the same as the subway and you can use a Metrocard or correct change ($2).

● Bus maps are available from token booth clerks in subway stations.

● Buses are safe, clean and excruciatingly slow. The fastest are Limited Stop buses.

● Ask the driver for a transfer that entitles you to a free onward or crosstown journey for an hour after boarding using the intersecting services listed on the back.

● A bus map is essential.

SUBWAY

● New York's subway system has 26 routes and 468 stations, many open 24 hours (those with a green globe outside are always staffed).

● To ride the subway you need a Metrocard, which you can refill. Unlimited ride Metrocards are also available; with these you must wait 18 minutes between swipes. Swipe the card to enter the turnstile.

● Many stations have separate entrances for up- and downtown services. Make sure you take a local train, not a restricted-stop express.

● Cars are air-conditioned in summer. There is often some service outage that is announced on notices in the stations and on the MTA website.

● Children under 44in (113cm) tall ride free.

● Transit information ☎ 718/330-1234

ⓘ 24 hours; www.mta.info

● Avoid the less populated subway lines at night. If you do ride at night, stay in the "off hour waiting area" until your train arrives.

TAXIS

● A yellow cab is vacant when the central number on the roof is illuminated and the "Off Duty" side lights are not.

● All cabs display current rates on the door, have a meter inside and can supply a printed receipt.

SUBWAY TIPS

● If your Metrocard didn't work, don't go to a different turnstile or you'll lose a fare. As the display says, you should "swipe again."

● Check the circular signs on the outside of the cars to make sure you're boarding the correct train. Often two lines share a platform.

● Look at the boards above your head to check whether you're on the Up- or Downtown side and/or on the Local or Express track.

TAXIS

Taxi Cab ☎ 347/750-7026

123 24 Hour Taxi
☎ 212/239-1011

Gold Taxi Brokers
☎ 212/268-8548

NY Taxi Worker
☎ 212/683-3084

Town Car Taxi Service
☎ 718/392-9805

NEED TO KNOW GETTING AROUND

BROOKLYN

If you're visiting friends or sights in Brooklyn, the same subway rules apply, but you may have to change trains since several local lines (1, 6, E, V, W) only operate in Manhattan (not Queens). No buses cross the bridges but you can pick up a Brooklyn bus map at subway stations.

VISITORS WITH DISABILITIES

City law requires that all facilities constructed after 1987 provide complete access to people with disabilities. Many owners of older buildings have willingly added disability-access features as well. Two important resources are the Mayor's Office for People with Disabilities (✉ 100 Gold Street, 2nd floor, 10038 ☎ 212/788-2830; www.nyc.gov/mopd) and Hospital Audiences' guide to New York's cultural institutions, *Access for All* (☎ 212/575-7676; www.hospitalaudiences.org). This $5 book describes the accessibility of each place, with information on hearing and visual aids, alternative entrances and the height of telephones and water fountains. H.A. also provides descriptions of theater performances on audio cassettes for people with visual impairments.

- Cab drivers are notorious for (a) knowing nothing about New York geography, (b) not speaking English and (c) having an improvisational driving style.
- Tip at least 15 percent. Bills larger than $10 are unpopular for short journeys.

DRIVING
- Driving in New York is not recommended, but a car is essential for excursions farther afield.
- The address of the nearest major car-rental outlet can be found by calling the following toll-free numbers:

Avis ☎ 800/331-1212
Budget ☎ 800/527-0700
Hertz ☎ 800/654-3131
National ☎ 800/227-7368

- If driving in New York is unavoidable, make sure you understand the restrictions because penalties for infringements are stringent.
- In many streets parking alternates daily from one side to the other and it is illegal to park within 10ft (3m) either side of a fire hydrant. A car illegally parked will be towed away and the driver heavily fined.
- Within the city limits right turns at a red light are prohibited and the speed limit is 30mph (48kph).
- Passing a stopped school bus is illegal and stiff fines can be imposed.

WALKING
New York is one of the few US cities in which the predominant mode of transportation is walking. Especially if the weather is cooperating (and if it isn't, umbrella vendors materialize on every other corner), it's far nicer to hike a 10- or 20-block distance than to descend below ground on the subway, or sit in a cab stalled in traffic. It's also often faster. To work it out for yourself, figure one minute per short block (north–south) and two per long block (east–west, on cross streets). New Yorkers tend to walk fast and there are few collisions.

Essential Facts

CUSTOMS
● Non-US citizens may import duty-free:
1 quart (just under a liter) of alcohol (no one under 21 can import alcohol), 200 cigarettes or 50 cigars and $100 of gifts.
● Have a doctor's certificate for any medication you are taking with you.
● Among restricted items for import are meat, fruit, plants, seeds and lottery tickets.

ELECTRICITY
● The supply is 100 volts, 60 cycles AC current.
● US appliances use two-prong plugs.
European appliances require an adapter.

ETIQUETTE
● Tipping: waitstaff get 15–20 percent (roughly double the 8.375 percent sales tax at the bottom of the bill); so do cab drivers. Bartenders get about the same (though less than $1 is stingy). Bellhops ($1 per bag), room service waiters (10 percent), and hairdressers (15–20 percent) should also be tipped.
● There are stringent smoking laws in New York. Smoking is banned on all public transportation, in cabs and in all places of work, including restaurants and bars.

MEDICAL TREATMENT
● It is essential to have adequate insurance.
● In the event of an emergency, the 911 operator will send an ambulance.
● Doctors on Call (24 hours) ☎ 212/737-1212
● Near Midtown, 24-hour emergency rooms: Roosevelt Hospital ⊠ 10th Avenue and 59th Street ☎ 212/523-4000
St. Vincent's Hospital ⊠ 7th Avenue/12th Street ☎ 212/604-7000
● Dental Emergency Service ⊠ 230 Park Avenue 1164 ☎ 212/682-5180

MEDICINES
● Several drugstores are open 24 hours.

VISITOR INFORMATION
● NYC & Company provides free bus and subway maps, calendars of events and discount coupons for Broadway shows ⊠ 810 7th Avenue ☎ 212/484-1222; www.nyc visit.com ◑ Mon–Fri 8.30–6, weekends 9–5. There are also information booths at City Hall Park, Federal Hall, Chinatown and Harlem. See website for details.
● Times Square Information Center also provides free maps, brochures, information and sells tickets for transport and entertainment ⊠ 1560 Broadway between 46th and 47th streets ☎ 212/768-1560; www.timessquarenyc.org ◑ Daily 8–8

EMERGENCY NUMBERS
● Police, Fire Department, Ambulance ☎ 911
● Crime Victims Hotline ☎ 212/577-7777
● Sex Crimes Report Line ☎ 212/267-7273

TOILETS
● Don't use public toilets on the street, in stations or in subways.
● Public buildings provide locked bathrooms (ask the doorman, cashier or receptionist for the key).
● Use toilets in hotel lobbies, bars or restaurants.

MONEY

The unit of currency is the dollar (= 100 cents). Notes (bills) come in denominations of $1, $5, $10, $20, $50 and $100; coins come in 25¢ (a quarter), 10¢ (a dime), 5¢ (a nickel) and 1¢ (a penny).

5 dollars

10 dollars

50 dollars

100 dollars

VISA AND TRAVEL INSURANCE

Check your insurance policy and buy a supplementary policy if needed. A minimum of $1 million medical cover is recommended. Choose a policy that also includes trip cancellation, baggage and document loss.

MONEY MATTERS

● Credit cards are widely accepted. Visa, MasterCard, American Express, Diner's Card and Discover are most commonly used.
● US dollar traveler's checks are often accepted in lieu of cash. It is difficult to exchange foreign currency traveler's checks, even at banks, and fees are high.

NEWSPAPERS AND MAGAZINES

● The local papers are the *New York Times* (with a huge Sunday edition), the *Daily News* (also with big Sunday supplements) and the *New York Post*. The free alternative paper the *Village Voice* has extensive listings. Also look for the respected *Wall Street Journal* and the pink-hued, gossip-heavy, weekly *New York Observer*.
● As well as the *New Yorker, New York* and *Time Out New York*, you may also see the hip *Paper*, the glossy *Manhattan File* and the even glossier *Avenue*.

OPENING HOURS

● Banks: Mon–Fri 9–3 or 3.30; some are open longer, and on Saturday.
● Stores: Mon–Sat 10–6; many are open far later, and on Sunday 12–6; those in the Villages, Nolita and SoHo open and close later.
● Museums: hours vary, but Monday is the most common closing day.
● Post offices: Mon–Fri 8 or 9–6. Some open Sat 9–4.

MAIL AND TELEPHONES

● The main post office ✉ 8th Avenue (33rd Street) ☎ 212/330-3002 is open 24 hours. Branch post offices are listed in Yellow Pages.
● Stamps are also available from hotel concierges, online at www.usps.com, at some delis and from vending machines in stores.
● All New York numbers require the prefix to be dialed (212, 718, 646, 347 or 917). For long-distance calls, add a "1" before the code.
● Hotels can levy hefty surcharges, even on

local calls, so use payphones instead or the long-distance services of AT&T, MCI and Sprint; typically, you dial an 800 number.

● Prepaid phonecards are widely available in stores, and there are a few credit card phones.

● To call the US from the UK, dial 001. To call the UK from the US, dial 011 44, then drop the first zero from the area code.

SENSIBLE PRECAUTIONS

● Maintain awareness of your surroundings and of other people, and try to look as though you know your way around.

● Don't get involved with street crazies, however entertaining they are.

● The less populated subway lines are best avoided at night and also certain areas of Brooklyn. Generally, areas of Manhattan that were once considered unsafe (Alphabet City east of Avenue C, the far west of Midtown, north of about 110th Street and Central Park) are far less edgy than they used to be. Still, keep your wits about you in deserted areas.

● Use common-sense rules: conceal your wallet; keep the fastener of your bag on the inside; and don't flash large amounts of cash or jewelry.

● New York women are streetwise and outspoken, so if you are a woman and someone's bugging you, tell him to get lost—he'll be expecting it.

RADIO AND TELEVISION

● New York's National Public Radio station, WNYC, broadcasts avant-garde and classical music, as well as jazz, news and cultural shows on FM 93.9 and AM 820.

● Air America's (WLIB 1190 AM) *Al Franken Show* and *Majority Report* with comedian Janeane Garofalo reflect New York's liberal bias, as does Comedy Central's hit *The Daily Show* with Jon Stewart on cable TV.

STUDENTS

● An International Student Identity Card (ISIC) is good for reduced admission at many museums, theaters and other attractions.

● Carry the ISIC or some other photo ID card at all times, to prove you're a fulltime student or over 21.

● Under-25s will find it hard to rent a car.

CONSULATES

Australia	✉ 636 5th Avenue	☎ 212/351-6500
Canada	✉ 1251 6th Avenue	☎ 212/596-1628
Denmark	✉ 885 2nd Avenue, 18th Floor	☎ 212/223-4545
France	✉ 934 5th Avenue	☎ 212/606-3600
Germany	✉ 871 UN Plaza	☎ 212/610-9700
Ireland	✉ 515 Madison Avenue	☎ 212/319-2555
Italy	✉ 690 Park Avenue	☎ 212/439-8600
Netherlands	✉ 1 Rockefeller Plaza	☎ 877/388-2443
Norway	✉ 825 3rd Avenue	☎ 212/421-7333
Sweden	✉ Dag Hammarskjöld Plaza	☎ 212/583-2550
UK	✉ 845 3rd Avenue	☎ 212/745-0200

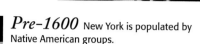

Timeline

THE FIGHT FOR INDEPENDENCE

In 1664 Wall Street's wall failed to deter the British, who invaded Manhattan Island and named it New York. Almost 100 years later, in 1763, the Treaty of Paris gave the British control over 13 American colonies. In 1770 the Sons of Liberty fought the British at the Battle of Golden Hill and in 1776 the American Revolutionary War began and the British chose New York as their headquarters. The Declaration of Independence was read at Bowling Green in July 1776 and the Treaty of Paris ended the war in 1783.

Pre–1600 New York is populated by Native American groups.

1609 Henry Hudson sails up the Hudson seeking the Northwest Passage.

1625 "Nieuw Amsterdam" is founded by the Dutch West India Company. A year later the colony's leader buys Manhattan Island from the Native Americans for $24 of trinkets.

1664 The British invade.

1776 American Revolutionary War begins.

1783 War ends. Two years later New York becomes capital of the United States.

1789 George Washington is sworn in as first US president at Federal Hall.

1790 Philadelphia becomes US capital.

1807 Robert Fulton launches his first steamboat, creating trade routes that make many New Yorkers' fortunes.

1827 Slavery in New York is abolished.

1848 Start of first great immigrant waves.

1861 New York backs the Union during the Civil War.

1868 The first "El" (elevated train) opens.

1886 The Statue of Liberty is unveiled.

1892 Ellis Island opens.

1904 New York's first subway opens.

1929 The Great Depression begins.

1933 Prohibition ends. Fiorello LaGuardia becomes mayor.

1954 Ellis Island is closed down.

1964 Race riots in Harlem and Brooklyn.

1975 A federal loan saves New York City from bankruptcy.

1990 David Dinkins, New York's first black mayor, takes office.

2001 Terrorists fly two hijacked passenger planes into the World Trade Center twin towers, destroying them and killing an estimated 3,000 people in the 9/11 tragedy.

2002 Rudy Giuliani's term as mayor ends. Michael Bloomberg takes office.

2004 New Yorkers vote overwhelmingly for presidential candidate John Kerry. President George W. Bush begins second term.

2007 Former mayor Giuliani enters the race for US President as a Republican candidate.

TENEMENT LIFE

As you make your first explorations in New York, consider how it was for the early immigrants, especially those who were herded through Ellis Island, then crammed into Lower East Side tenements. Imagine how daunting the cast iron-framed SoHo buildings must have appeared to someone from, say, Vienna. Although they are now the scene of costly loft living, or home to chain stores or swank boutiques, during the immigrant boom they were sweatshop skyscrapers–symbols of hope for a fresh future.

An early view of the Bay of New York (far left); Customs House, New York (left); Brooklyn Bridge in the 19th century (below right); modern-day transportation on the subway (below)

Index

New York City's
25 BEST

WRITTEN BY Kate Sekules
DESIGN WORK Jacqueline Bailey
COVER DESIGN Tigist Getachew
INDEXER Marie Lorimer
IMAGE RETOUCHING AND REPRO Michael Moody, Sarah Montgomery
REVIEWING EDITOR Paul Eisenberg

UPDATED BY Donna Dailey

© AA Media Limited 2009 (registered office: Fanum House, Basing View, Basingstoke, Hampshire RG21 4EA, registered number 06112600).

Reprinted July 2009

ISBN 978-1-4000-0790-5

EIGHTH EDITION

IMPORTANT TIP
Time inevitably brings changes, so always confirm prices, travel facts, and other perishable information when it matters. Although Fodor's cannot accept responsibility for errors, you can use this guide in the confidence that we have taken every care to ensure its accuracy.

SPECIAL SALES
This book is available for special discounts for bulk purchases for sales promotions or premiums. Special editions, including personalized covers, excerpts of existing books, and corporate imprints, can be created in large quantities for special needs. For more information, write to Special Markets/Premium Sales, 1745 Broadway, MD 6–2, New York, NY 10019 or email specialmarkets@randomhouse.com.

Color separation by Keenes, Andover, UK
Printed and bound by Leo Paper Products, China
10 9 8 7 6 5 4 3 2

A04227
Maps in this title produced from map data © Tele Atlas N.V. 2007   Tele Atlas
Transport map © Communicarta Ltd, UK

The Automobile Association would like to thank the following photographers, companies and picture libraries for their assistance in the preparation of this book.

Abbreviations for the picture credits are as follows – (t) top; (b) bottom; (c) centre; (l) left; (r) right; (AA) AA World Travel Library.

1 AA/C Sawyer; **2/3t** AA/C Sawyer; **4/5t** AA/C Sawyer; **4tl** AA/C Sawyer; **5** AA/C Sawyer; **6/7t** AA/C Sawyer; **6cl** AA/S McBride; **6c** AA/C Sawyer; **6cr** AA/C Sawyer; **6bl** AA/S McBride; **6br** AA/S McBride; **7cl** AA/C Sawyer; **7c** AA/C Sawyer; **7cr** AA/C Sawyer; **7bl** AA/C Sawyer; **7bc** AA/D Corrance; **7br** AA/C Sawyer; **8/9t** AA/C Sawyer; **10/11** AA/C Sawyer; **10tr** AA/C Sawyer; **10ctr** AA/C Sawyer; **10cbr** AA/C Sawyer; **10br** AA/ M Jourdan; **11tl** AA/ C Sawyer; **11ctl** AA/S McBride; **11c** AA/C Sawyer; **11cbl** AA/C Sawyer; **11bl** AA/C Sawyer; **12/13t** AA/C Sawyer; **12b** AA/C Sawyer; **13tl** AA/C Sawyer; **13ctl** AA/C Sawyer; **13c** Photodisc; **13cbl** Brand X pics; **13bl** AA/C Sawyer; **14/5t** AA/C Sawyer; **14tr** AA/C Sawyer; **14tcr** AA/P Kenward; **14c** AA/C Sawyer; **14bcr** AA/C Sawyer;**14br** AA/S McBride; **15b** AA/S McBride; **16/7t** AA/C Sawyer; **16t** Photodisc; **16c** AA/R Elliot; **16b** AA/C Sawyer; **17t** AA/S McBride; **17tc** AA/S McBride; **17bc** AA; **17b** AA/C Sawyer; **18t** AA/C Sawyer; **18tc** AA/R Elliot; **18c** AA/D Corrance; **18cb** AA/P Kenward; **18b** AA/S Collier; **19(I)** AA/C Sawyer; **19(II)** AA/S McBride; **19(III)** AA/C Sawyer; **19(IV)** AA/C Sawyer; **19(V)** AA/C Sawyer; **19(VI)** AA/C Sawyer; **20/1** AA/S McBride; **24tl** AA/C Sawyer; **24tr** AA/C Sawyer; **25tl** AA/C Sawyer; **25tr** AA/S McBride; **26l** AA/C Sawyer; **26/7t** AA/R Elliot; **26/7b**; AA/C Sawyer; **27r** AA/C Sawyer; **28l** AA/C Sawyer; **28r** AA/C Sawyer; **29t** AA/C Sawyer; **29bl** AA/C Sawyer; **29br** AA/C Sawyer; **30t** AA/C Sawyer; **30bl** AA/C Sawyer; **30br** AA/C Sawyer; **31t** AA/C Sawyer; **32t** AA/C Sawyer; **33t** AA/S McBride; **34t** AA/C Sawyer; **35** AA/C Sawyer; **38tl** AA/S McBride; **38bl** AA/C Sawyer; **38/9t** AA/S McBride; **38br** AA/C Sawyer; **38/9br** AA/C Sawyer; **39r** AA/C Sawyer; **40tl** AA/S McBride; **40tc** AA/S McBride; **40tr** AA/S McBride; **41tl** AA/C Sawyer; **41tr** AA/C Sawyer; **42/3t** AA/C Sawyer; **42bl** AA/C Sawyer; **42br** AA/C Sawyer; **43bl** AA/C Sawyer; **43br** AA/C Sawyer; **44t** AA/C Sawyer; **45t** AA/C Sawyer; **46t** Digitalvision; **47** AA/S McBride; **48t** AA/C Sawyer; **49** AA/C Sawyer; **52tl** AA/C Sawyer; **52/3t** AA/S McBride; **53tr** AA/R Elliot; **54tl** AA/S McBride; **54/5t** AA/R Elliot; **54br** AA/D Corrance; **54/5b** AA/C Sawyer; **55r** AA/C Sawyer; **56** AA/C Sawyer; **56/7** AA/C Sawyer; **58/9** AA/S McBride; **59t** AA/S McBride; **59bl** AA/S McBride; **59br** AA/S McBride; **60tl** 2006 Timothy Hursley/MOMA; **60tc** 2005 Timothy Hursley/MOMA; **60tr** 2005 Timothy Hursley/ MOMA; **61tl** AA/R Elliot; **61tr** AA; **62tl** AA/C Sawyer; **62tc** AA/C Sawyer; **62tr** AA/C Sawyer; **63tl** AA/S McBride; **63tr** AA/C Sawyer; **64tl** AA/C Sawyer; **64tr** AA/C Sawyer; **65t** AA/C Sawyer; **65b** Norman McGrath/ International Center of Photography; **66t** AA/C Sawyer; **66bl** AA/D Corrance; **66br** AA/C Sawyer; **67t** AA/C Sawyer; **68t** AA/C Sawyer; **69t** AA/C Sawyer; **70t** AA/S McBride; **71** AA/C Sawyer; **74tl** AA/P Kenward; **74/5tc** AA/S McBride; **74bl** AA/P Kenward; **74br** AA/C Sawyer; **75tr** AA/S McBride; **74/5b** AA/C Sawyer; **75br** AA/P Kenward; **76tl** AA/C Sawyer; **76tr** AA/C Sawyer; **77tl** The Frick Collection/Galen Lee; **77tr** John Bigelow Taylor/The Frick Collection; **78/9tl** AA/S McBride; **79tr** AA/C Sawyer; **79br** AA/C Sawyer; **80/1tl** AA/C Sawyer; **81tr** AA/R Elliot; **82/3** AA/P Kenward; **84t** AA/C Sawyer; **84bl** AA/C Sawyer; **84br** Harry Zernike / Museum of the City of NY; **85t** AA/C Sawyer; **86t** AA/C Sawyer; **87** AA/P Kenward; **88t** AA/C Sawyer; **89** AA/P Kenward; **92t** AA/C Sawyer; **92/3t** AA/E Rooney; **94/5t** AA/C Sawyer; **95t** AA/C Sawyer; **96t** AA/C Sawyer; **97t** AA/C Sawyer; **98** AA/P Kenward; **99t** AA/P Kenward; **100t** AA/S McBride; **101** AA/C Sawyer; **104t** AA/Nicky Lancaster; **104/5t** AA/C Sawyer; **106/7t** AA/C Sawyer; **106bl** AA/C Sawyer; **106br** AA/P Kenward; **107bl** AA/R Elliot; **107br** AA/C Sawyer; **108t** AA/S McBride; **109** AA/C Sawyer; **110/11t** AA/C Sawyer; **110tr** AA/C Sawyer; **110ctr** AA/C Sawyer; **110cbr** AA/C Sawyer; **110br** AA/C Sawyer; **112/3** AA/C Sawyer; **114t** AA/C Sawyer; **115** AA/S McBride; **116/7t** AA/D Corrance; **118/9t** AA/D Corrance; **120/1t** AA/D Corrance; **122/3t** AA/D Corrance; **122c** MRI Bankers' Guide to Foreign Currency, Houston, USA; **122b** AA/C Sawyer; **124/5t** AA/D Corrance; **124bl** AA; **124br** AA; **125bl** AA; **125br** AA/C Sawyer.

Every effort has been made to trace the copyright holders, and we apologise in advance for any accidental errors. We would be happy to apply the corrections in the following edition of this publication.